GREAT CAMPAIGNS

The Spotsylvania Campaign

GREAT CAMPAIGN SERIES

The Antietam Campaign
The Appomattox Campaign
The Atlanta Campaign
The Chancellorsville Campaign
The First Air Campaign
The Gettysburg Campaign
Jackson's Valley Campaign
The Little Bighorn Campaign
MacArthur's New Guinea Campaign
The Midway Campaign
The Peninsula Campaign
The Petersburg Campaign
The Philadelphia Campaign
Rommel's North Africa Campaign
The Second Bull Run Campaign
The Shiloh Campaign
The Spotsylvania Campaign
The Vicksburg Campaign
The Waterloo Campaign
The Wilderness Campaign

GREAT CAMPAIGNS

THE SPOTSYLVANIA CAMPAIGN

May 7 - 21, 1864

John Cannan

COMBINED BOOKS
Pennsylvania

PUBLISHER'S NOTE

The headquarters of Combined Publishing are located midway between Valley Forge and the Germantown battlefield, on the outskirts of Philadelphia. From its beginnings, our company has been steeped in the oldest traditions of American military history and publishing. Our historic surroundings help maintain our focus on military history and our books strive to uphold the standards of style, quality and durability first established by the earliest bookmakers of Germantown and Philadelphia so many years ago. Our famous monk-and-console logo reflects our commitment to the modern and yet historic enterprise of publishing.

We call ourselves Combined Publishing because we have always felt that our goals could only be achieved through a "combined" effort by authors, publishers and readers. We have always tried to maintain maximum communication between these three key players in the reading experience.

We are always interested in hearing from prospective authors about new books in our field. We also like to hear from our readers and invite you to contact us at our offices in Pennsylvania with any questions, comments or suggestions, or if you have difficulty finding our books at a local bookseller.

For information, address:
Combined Publishing
1024 Fayette Street
P.O. Box 307
Conshohocken, PA 19428
E-mail: combined@dca.net
Web: www.dca.net/combinedbooks
Orders: 1-800-4-1860-65

Library of Congress Cataloging-in-Publication Data available.
Cannan, John, 1967-
    The Spotsylvania campaign : May 7-21, 1864 / John Cannan.
        p.   cm. -- (Great campaigns)
    Includes bibliographical references (p.) and index.
    ISBN 0-938289-47-0
    1. Spotsylvania Court House, Battle of, Va., 1864.   I. Series.
E476.52.C35   1997
973.7'36--dc21   97-31902
                                                                        CIP

Printed in the United States of America.
Maps by Paul Dangel.

Contents

Sidebars

Maps

Preface to the Series

*J*onathan Swift termed war "that mad game the world so loves to play." He had a point. Universally condemned, it has nevertheless been almost as universally practiced. For good or ill, war has played a significant role in the shaping of history. Indeed, there is hardly any human institution which has not in some fashion been influenced and molded by war, even as it helped shape and mold war in turn. Yet the study of war has been as remarkably neglected as its practice has been commonplace. With a few outstanding exceptions, the history of wars and of military operations has until quite recently been largely the province of the inspired patriot or the regimental polemicist. Only in our times have serious, detailed, and objective accounts come to be considered the norm in the treatment of military history and related matters.

Yet there still remains a gap in the literature, for there are two types of military history. One type is written from a very serious, hightly techinical, professional perspective and presupposes that the reader is deeply familiar with background, technology, and general situation. The other is perhaps less dry, but merely lightly reviews the events with the intention of informing and entertaining the layperson. The qualitative gap between the two is vast. Moreover, there are professionals in both the military and in academia whose credentials are limited to particular moments in the long, sad history of war, and there are interested readers who have a more than passing under-

9

standing of the field; and then there is the concerned citizen, interested in understanding the phenomenon in an age of unusual violence and unprecedented armaments. It is to bridge the gap betwen the two types of military history, and to reach the professional and the serious amateur and the concerned citizen alike, that this series, *The Great Campaigns of Military History*, is designed.

The individual volumes of *The Great Campaigns of Military History* are each devoted to an intensive examination of a particularly significant military operation. The focus is not on individual battles, but on campaigns, on the relationship between movements and battles and how they fit within the overall framework of the war in question. By making use of a series of innovative techniques for the presentation of information, *The Great Campaigns of Military History* can satisfy the exacting demands of the professional and the serious amateur, while making it possible for the concerned citizen to understand the events and the condtions under which they developed. This is accomplished in a number of ways. Each volume contains a substantial, straight-forward narrative account of the campaign under study. This is supported by an extensive series of modular "side-bars." Some are devoted to particular specific technical matters, such as weaponry, logistics, organization, or tactics. These modules each contain detailed analyses of their topic, and make considerable use of "hard" data, with many charts and tables. Other modules deal with less technical matters, such as strategic analyses, anecdotes, personalities, uniforms, and politics. Each volume contains several detailed maps, supplemented by a number of clear, accurate sketch-maps, which assist the reader in understanding the course of events under consideration, and there is an extensive set of illustrations which have been selected to assist the reader still further. Finally, each volume contains materials designed to help the reader who is interested in learning more. But this "bibliography" includes not merely a short list of books and articles related to the campaign in question. It also contains information on study groups devoted to the subject, on films which deal with it, on recordings of period music, on simulation games and skirmish clubs which attempt to recreate the tactics, on museums where one can have a first-hand look at equipment, and on tours of the battlefields. The particular contents of each volume will, of course, be determined by the topic in question, but each will provide an unusually rich and varied treatment of the subject. Each volume in *The Great Campaigns of Military History* is thus not merely an account of a particular military operation, but it is a unique reference to the theory and practice of war in the period in question.

The Great Campaigns of Military History is a unique contribution to the study of war and of military history, which will remain of interest and use for many years.

CHAPTER I

Grant on the Move

7-8 May 1864

*U*lysses S. Grant came to Washington in early 1864 to take command of all the Union armies, a position attained by becoming the Union's foremost general and greatest hero, with a battle record that included many of the North's most signal victories of the war, such as Shiloh, Vicksburg, and Chattanooga. Still, there was great uncertainty and even skepticism that Lieutenant General Grant would ever be a match for the South's greatest commander, General Robert E. Lee, the masterful commander of the Army of Northern Virginia, who had made his legendary reputation by destroying the careers of several Northern opponents. The question of whether or not Grant would equal Lee was put to the test in May 1864 when Grant launched his first offensive in the East. From 5-6 May, the lieutenant general had the *Army of the Potomac* under Major General George Gordon Meade pound Lee's army in the thick cheerless woodland of the Wilderness, 10 miles west of Fredricksburg, Virginia. The combat there was intense, the casualties heavy, but the result inconsequential. Charge and counter charge were stalemated, blows were parried by regiments, brigades, divisions and corps. The battlefield itself was left a grisly inferno, choked by smoke from fires that consumed brush

Eastern Theater
Of Operations
1864

By May, 1864, Ulysses S. Grant was in su-preme command of the Union armies, while personally accompanying the **Army of the Potomac** *in the field.*

and the flesh of the dead and wounded. Horace Porter, staff officer to Grant, applied all the literary skill at his command to describe the awful carnage on the Wilderness battlefield in his classic memoirs, *Campaigning With Grant*:

> All circumstances seemed to combine to make the scene one of unutterable horror. At times the wind howled through the tree-tops, mingling its moans with the groans of the dying, and heavy branches were cut off by the fire of the artillery, and fell crashing upon the heads of men, adding a new terror to the battle. Forest fires raged; ammunition-trains exploded; the dead

were roasted in the conflagration; the wounded roused by its hot breath, dragged themselves along, with their torn and mangled limbs, in the mad energy of despair, to escape the ravages of the flames; and every bush seemed hung with the shreds of blood-stained clothing. It was as though Christian men had turned to fiends, and hell itself had usurped the place of earth.

Here, at the Wilderness, Grant had proven at least a match for Lee, yet neither he nor his opponent had been able to gain an advantage or a reason to call this painful fight a victory. Now there was a question for both men to answer, what to do next?

With both armies remaining passive on 7 May, soldiers on either side could turn their attention to matters besides fighting. Thousands of men lay dead on the field itself or in hospitals awaiting a rude burial. One soldier wrote of the grim lack of ceremony given to the fallen, "At best the work was very imperfectly done, and hundreds of comrades with blankets or shelter-tents for winding-sheets were placed in shallow trenches scarcely deep enough to cover their remains." The treatment was even worse for the enemy dead as another recalled, "There is very little ceremony in burying the dead of an enemy. With a shovel the dirt is removed the length of the soldier and to a depth of eight to ten inches, and then with the shovel the body is turned into the little trench, sometimes falling on side or back and sometimes on the face; the dirt removed from the trench is the shoveled onto the body, and is washed off by the rains, when the body is mutilated by hogs or vultures." A legion of wounded also had to be attended to. Many of these were scarred for life by injuries from minie ball, cannon shell, or canister, wounds requiring amputation of a limb under the surgeon's saw. One Federal soldier making his way to hospitals at Fredericksburg saw many a pitiful scene as a wagon train of wounded passed him, "Many of the poor boys die in the ambulances while going over the rough corduroy roads. It was heart rending to hear their groans and cries for water without being able to help them. Those who were able to walk considered themselves lucky." As awful as these scenes were, many more loomed in the future.

All this death and all these battle scars were the fruits of a battle Grant had originally intended to avoid. He had hoped that after his army crossed the Rapidan River into the Wilderness on 4 May, he could get his troops to march quickly through the forest toward a more suitable place for a confrontation, perhaps on open ground where his greater strength in numbers might be used for great effect. When the Confederates showed themselves in the Wilderness, Grant decided to fight at a heavy price of 17,666 casualties for no real gain. None of Grant's defeated predecessors had suffered so terribly in an engagement across the Rapidan.

Abraham Lincoln, President of the United States, had once said of Grant, "I can't spare this man, he fights." And this quality of the general's would be displayed in the face of his costly stalemate in the Wilderness. Despite his considerable losses the Western general was not prepared to admit defeat, or consider the prospect of retreating as former commanders of the *Army of the Potomac* had done. His only thoughts were of moving forward, of pondering the possibility of finding a field where he would have a greater opportunity to best his foe. Grant informed his staff of his intent to remain on the offensive, putting a positive spin on the situation thus far and his hopes for a more successful result in the future,

> While it is in one sense a drawn battle, as neither side has gained or lost ground substantially since the fighting began, yet we remain in possession of the field, and the forces opposed to us have withdrawn to a distance from our front and taken up a defensive position. We cannot call the engagement a positive victory, but the enemy have only twice actually reached our lines in their many attacks, and have not gained a single advantage. This will enable me to carry out my intention of moving to the left, and compelling the enemy to fight in a more open country outside of their breastworks.

This desire for a fight on open ground was only one consideration for Grant. There were other considerations affecting his planning that would have their impact felt on other Union offensives many miles away.

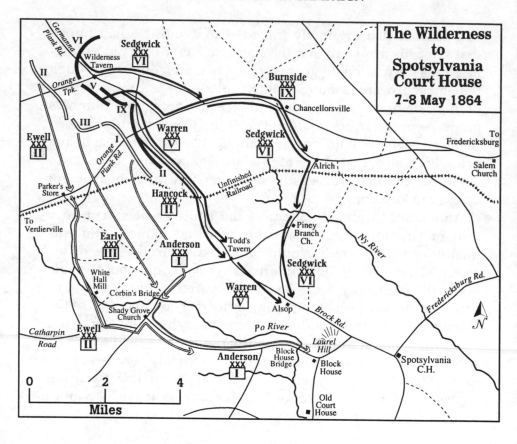

The Wilderness to Spotsylvania Court House 7-8 May 1864

While the *Army of the Potomac* engaged Lee, Major General Benjamin Butler was involved in another Union operation farther south against the Confederate capital of Richmond. Grant learned on 7 May that this offensive was already beginning to yield success as Butler had taken City Point, a critical position on the James River on the way to Richmond. But this good news also contained a dangerous portent; if Butler became too successful Lee might detach himself from facing Grant and come to Richmond's defense and threaten the aggressive Yankee army there with annihilation. It was essential then for the *Army of the Potomac* to keep Bobbie Lee occupied north of Richmond.

The best way to compel Lee to battle on Grant's own terms was to get between his army and the Confederate capital. To do this, Grant decided to move his army around 12 miles southeast of his current position towards the crossroads town of Spotsylvania Court House, right on an important supply route for the Confederate army as well as a point on the road to Richmond. With the Federal army there, Lee could somehow be forced either to fight out in the open on Grant's terms or retreat further south.

On 7 May, the battered *Army of the Potomac* was in a line roughly following the Brock Road, one of the few good routes through the Wilderness running southeast from Germanna Ford. Major General John Sedgwick's *VI Corps* on the right flank bulged out to the west, followed in line by Major General Gouverneur Warren's *V Corps* and Major General Ambrose Burnside's *IX Corps*, projecting west astride the Orange Turnpike. The *II Corps* on the left, entrenched along the Brock Road, held the left by extending to the southeast.

Early on 7 May, at 0630, Grant issued an order for the *Army of the Potomac's* move from these positions toward Spotsylvania. Preparations were to be made for a night march down the Brock Road for the Court House with one army corps while another was to head for Todd's Tavern and another for a position near the intersection of the Piney Branch and Spotsylvania roads with the road from Alsop's to Old Court House. Grant advised letting Gouverneur Warren's *V Corps* make the march down the

*George G. Meade's volatile temperament
was not helped by the difficulty of commanding the* **Army of the Potomac** *with his com-
mander-in-chief traveling with him.*

Brock Road to Spotsylvania, moving behind Hancock's command, which would follow later to become the right of the new
line. Sedgwick's *VI Corps* was to make for its destination via
Chancellorsville with Burnside following in his wake. All vehi-
cles in the *Army of the Potomac* were to be taken out of listening
distance of the enemy before the troops marched and hospitals
were to be moved that day to Chancellorsville. Grant noted the
possibility of a modification to his orders should the enemy
attack in the afternoon. Meade was told to be prepared to offer
resistance, and follow up any success gained, with the entire
army.

Grant's orders made their way through the cumbersome
command structure of the *Army of the Potomac*, an odd arrange-

By spring, 1864, the **Army of the Potomac** *had a cumbersome wagon train, but it contained sophisticated workshops which could build or repair bridges, railroads, gun mountings and wagons.*

ment that had come into being when the Western commander took control in the East. As general in chief of all the Federal armies, Grant was in command of the forces both in the East and West, 745,000 troops in 19 military districts. While his predecessor in the post, Major General Henry W. Halleck, had managed his affairs in Washington, Grant chose to travel with the *Army of the Potomac,* then under George Gordon Meade. Grant claimed Meade was given a free hand to direct the army's affairs, perhaps an unrealistic claim for, inevitably, he often saw fit to exert substantial influence over the *Army of the Potomac*'s movements, the 7 May planning for its next offensive being a prime example. This direct interference with the handling of the *Army of the Potomac* effectively gave it two commanders unequal in power: Grant the superior and Meade, effectively a subordinate in the army he led, the mere executor of Grant's directives.

*The Orange Plank Road in 1864, one of
the better roads in northern Virginia.*

Compounding the confusion was the fact that Burnside's *IX Corps* was allowed to act as an independent force from the *Army of the Potomac* while serving with it. Orders for its movements came from Grant, not Meade. This arrangement had already proven a difficult affair to manage in the Wilderness and its problems would continue into the Spotsylvania operation.

Meade, true to his role as a subordinate, followed Grant's directions, issuing specific orders at 1500 with instructions to all elements of his command for the advance toward Spotsylvania. The cumbersome wagon trains of the *Army of the Potomac* were to get in motion for Chancellorsville at 1600 to clear the way for the troops. The *Reserve Artillery* would be sent to Chancellorsville as well at 1900 and were then to move further to the rear to make way for the *VI Corps*. The responsibility for leading off the infantry movement fell upon Warren's *V Corps*, ordered to move south at 2030 down the Brock Road via Todd's Tavern for Spotsylvania, passing behind the *IX* and *II Corps*. Next, the *VI Corps* would get on the Orange Turnpike and the Orange Plank Road for Chancellorsville and move south for the intersection of the Piney Branch Church and Spotsylvania Road with a route leading from Alsop's to Old Court House. The *II Corps* would maintain its position to safeguard the movements of the rest of the army and then follow the *V Corps* route south. The cavalry under Major General Philip Sheridan was to have sufficient force on the Federal right to detect any approach of an enemy force. Burnside's *IX Corps* would participate in the *Army of the Potomac*'s movement by following the *VI Corps* route to Chancellorsville via the Germanna Plank Road to the Orange Plank Road and then south for Piney Branch Church.

Sheridan's cavalry was already in action early on the 7th around Todd's Tavern scattering Confederate troopers in position there. Around noon, Brigadier Generals Wesley Merritt's and David Gregg's cavalry divisions advanced south down the Brock Road with the objective of clearing a path for the general infantry movement. Brigadier James H. Wilson's division, battered after nearly being cut off from the rest of the army during the Wilderness battle, would enjoy restful duty guarding the trains at Chancellorsville. Opposing Merritt and Gregg were two of Jeb Stuart's Confederate cavalry divisions near Todd's Tavern, one under Major General Wade Hampton and the other under Major General Fitzhugh Lee. The afternoon of 7 May was filled with the flash of sabres and crackling of carbine fire as mounted and dismounted troopers on both sides engaged in charge and countercharge. The Federals finally got the upper hand and drove their foe down the Brock Road until darkness came, bringing an end to the fighting. Despite the day's gains, Sheridan's troops fell back over the ground they had fought over all day to go into bivouac near Todd's Tavern.

The infantry movement started off as darkness slowly crept across the sky with *V Corps* troops of Brigadier General John C. Robinson's, Brigadier Charles Griffin's, Brigadier Lysander Cutler's and Brigadier Samuel Crawford's divisions pulling back

The **Army of the Potomac's** *march from the Wilderness to Spotsylvania was long and dusty, but the men were marching southward, and not retreating.*

from their battlefield line, getting on the Brock Road and then heading south. The very fact the army was heading south was almost as heartening to the Union troops as a battlefield victory. The army was continuing its advance, instead of retreating as had been done in earlier fights with similar results, thus making their tremendous hardships and sacrifices and deaths of comrades seem in vain. All was different now that a new commander was in charge. William B. Lapham of the *7th Maine* jubilantly thought so when he and his comrades found out they would be moving forward, "I only judge others by myself, and I was truly happy we were advancing, which indicated that we had not been beaten. The rank and file of the army wanted no more retreating, and from the moment when we passed the roads that led to the Rappahannock fords and continued straight on toward Spotsylvania, I never had a doubt that General Grant would lead us on to final victory." A demonstration of this newly found optimism in the rank and file was made before General Grant himself. The lieutenant general and Meade left their headquarters to join the advance around 2100, riding past *V Corps* troops just as they began to head south on the Brock Road. Horace Porter saw the troops give their leaders a tremendous outburst of enthusiasm:

Soldier's weary and sleepy after their long battle, with stiffened limbs and smarting wounds, now sprang to their feet, forgetful of their pains, and rushed forward to the roadside. Wild cheers echoed through the forest, and glad shouts of triumph rent the air. Men swung their hats, tossed up their arms, and pressed forward to within touch of their chief, clapping their hands, and speaking to him with the familiarity of comrades. Pine-knots and leaves were set on fire, and lighted the scene with their weird flickering glare. The night march and become a triumphal procession for the new commander. The demonstration was the emphatic verdict pronounced by the troops upon his first battle in the East. The excitement had been imparted to the horses which soon became restive, and even the general's large bay... became difficult to manage. Instead of being elated by this significant ovation, the general, thoughtful only of the practical question of the success of the movement, said: "This is most unfortunate. The sound will reach the ears of the enemy, and I fear it may reveal our movement." By his direction, staff-officers rode forward and urged the men to keep quiet so as not to attract the enemy's attention; but the demonstration did not really cease until the general was out of sight.

The jubilation over the move also caused some soldiers to exhibit sour opinions about Meade's apparent usefulness. Soldiers were heard to say, "General Meade is nothing, but an adjutant for General Grant" or "I'm more account with my musket than he is now" or "They don't notice him so much as they do the orderlies." A soldier of the *11th New Jersey* confirmed this feeling, "The impression among the officers and men no doubt was pretty general that a retreat of the army across the Rapidan would be ordered, as it had been the custom in the past to fight a battle and then retreat, and it was not unreasonable to suppose that this would be repeated when the order came from General Grant to move toward Spotsylvania Court House. The boys made up their minds, that Meade's and Lee's express route as they called it was to be abandoned, and that Grant proposed to establish an office near Richmond." While others measured Meade's significance, staff officer Theodore Lyman took a moment to ponder the awe inspiring spectacle that was taking place, "It was a sultry night—no rain for many days; the horses hoofs raised intolerable clouds of dust, which, in this sandy region, is fine almost like flour. I never saw—nobody could see—a more striking spectacle than that road as we passed slowly along. All the way was a continuous low breastwork behind which lay crowded the sleeping infantry. They were so close as almost to be on top of each other; every man with his loaded musket in his hand, or lying at his side. A few yards outside stood a line of sentries, their muskets cocked,and others sat on top of the breastwork. Few of the officers allowed themselves any rest, but paced up and down, in their greatcoats and slouched hats, looking sharply after the sentries." Despite the enthusiasm of the troops and the epic grandeur of the movement, it quickly appeared as though the *Army of the Potomac* could not attain the speed Federal commanders had hoped for in order to attain success.

The march was excruciating. Troops, weary from days of heavy fighting, trudged through thick choking clouds of smoke from the remaining forest fires caused by the Wilderness battle, which was mixed with dust kicked up by their own marching. The columns of men jerked along in a persistent series of starts and stops seemingly calculated to aggravate their weariness. Some of these delays were unnecessarily caused by the very generals who were impressed with the need for quickness. After being cheered by their troops, Grant and Meade went on to visit Hancock's headquarters at the intersection of the Brock and Orange Plank roads where they would wait for the marching *V Corps* columns. At 2230, Warren's lead division, Robinson's, reached the intersection only to be held up by Meade's provost guard blocking the way. Grant and Meade decided to open the path by riding onward for Todd's Tavern. On the way, a wrong turn nearly took them into enemy lines, a mistake only avoided by staff officer Colonel C.B. Comstock's instinct as an engineer, which told him something was wrong and sent him ahead alone where he discovered enemy troops on the move. Retracing their steps, Grant, Meade and their staffs made their way to safety and bivouacked near Todd's Tavern around 2400.

Once at Todd's Tavern, more potential roadblocks to the *V Corps* advance were discovered: Gregg's cavalry division which was encamped there and Merritt's division a mile further south, both awaiting orders. A furious Meade issued instructions to the cavalry commanders to get them out of the way. One order for Merritt directed him to move his command south on the Brock Road, securing the route for Warren's troops. Merritt was then to place a brigade west of Spotsylvania at Block House to guard the routes leading to both crossroads towns while using his other two to cover the army's supply trains. Meade's order for Gregg had that general move to the vicinity of Corbin's Bridge where he was to watch the roads from Parker's Store. When the *II Corps* reached Todd's Tavern, Gregg was to send a force up the Brock Road back to Todd's Tavern to detect the approach of any Confederates that might be pursuing Hancock. After making these orders, Meade then notified the cavalry commander, Sheridan, of what he had done.

Warren reached Todd's Tavern around 0100 on 8 May to find headquarters and its escort again blocking his path and again he had to wait until they were moved. While this was being done, Warren met with Meade and was informed of the latter's orders to Merritt to clear the road for the *V Corps* advance. Warren had Robinson begin his march again after headquarters had moved out of the way while he went ahead to see about Merritt's progress, reaching that commander's position at 0300. What he found did not bode well: there was still an obstacle facing his troops since Merritt's cavalry division was only now making preparations for moving out. While Warren waited for the cavalry troopers to get on their way, his soldiers started arriving in tired masses and dropping to sleep almost as soon as they halted. The *V Corps* commander decided not to press matters and let his fatigued troops rest while Merritt got on his way. His corps would not be on the move again until 0600.

The other elements of the *Army of the Potomac* were also tardy in their movements. The *VI Corps* got under way about an hour late at 2130 and reached Chancellorsville around 0430 the next day. It then began its march for the intersection of the Piney Branch Church and Spotsylvania Road with the road from Alsop's to Old Court House. The advance south sparked hope in the ranks as it had in *V Corps*, though some turned to more ominous reflection as Pennsylvanian Harold C. George noted, "The rank and file of the Army of the Potomac of course were glad to get away from the deeply hated Wilderness but seemed depressed by the heavy losses we had sustained and had the conviction that in the two day of battles our army had gotten the worst in the fight." The march was also plagued by the elements that had made Warren's advance difficult, heat, smoke and continual starts and stops. Yankee Mason Tyler remembered, "It was a night of sweltering heat. No rain had fallen for several days, and the many wheels and feet of the horses and men pounded the dry soil into impalpable dust."

The *II Corps* was not able to move until daylight, since its path was blocked all night by Warren's men. After it was finally on the march, soldiers of the *152d New York* ran into a fallen enemy soldier near Todd's Tavern racked by agony and anger against his enemies. A unit historian wrote, "Here we saw a wounded rebel lying near the road and in the last agony of death. He was a tall man with long hair falling over his shoulders, a true type of a son of the south. Amid the most agonizing shrieks and groans, he would utter the most bitter imprecations and violent curses upon the Yankees that man could invent."

The last Union corps to leave the Wilderness field was Burnside's *IX Corps*, which massed at the Wilderness tavern while waiting for the *VI Corps* to finish its preparations for the move south. Early in the morning of 8 May, Burnside's troops proceeded to Chancellorsville and then went on to Alrich's where it stopped to rest. This left them on the field of the old Chancellorsville battleground where Lee had sparred with Major General Joseph Hooker the previous May. Some Federals paused to investigate the year-old battlefield litter to satisfy the whims of their morbid curiosity. Their searches led them over a ghostly ground with small mounds built by soldiers to cover the remains of their fallen comrades, causing some to reflect over an awful fate of war, as one recalled, "We all knew what was in each of those mounds, and when we stopped to think, it made our hearts sad to know that the graves of those men would soon be unknown." Many soldiers who died at Chancellorsville had not been so fortunate to enjoy even a shallow grave. Bones and even whole skeletons were scattered about giving the area a grotesquely chilling effect. Some Yankees were attracted with grim curiosity to an abnormally large skull and tried to find a cap that might fit over it.

While the Federals prepared to make their march south, loud and frightening roars came from the enemy's position, a series of huge bellowing cheers that bespoke defiance. The Rebel Yell was raised by Southern soldier after soldier from the extreme right of the Confederate line, and carried down the ranks to the other end of the army. A Confederate soldier wrote of the spectacle, "...at first [the Rebel Yell] heard like the rumbling of a distant train, it came rushing down the lines like the surging waves upon the ocean, increasing in loudness and grandeur; and passing, it would be heard dying on the left in the distance. Again it was heard coming from the right to die away again on the distant left. It was renewed three times, each time with increased vigor. It was a yell like the defiant tones of the thunderstorm, echoing and reechoing." The enemy was still spoiling for a fight and was preparing to find one.

The Army of Northern Virginia's position after the Wilderness battle had the left held by Major General Richard Ewell's Second Corps, bent back from the Culpeper Mine Road southwest to the Orange Turnpike where it headed south. It joined with Major General Ambrose P. Hill's Third Corps, part of which veered east to join with the First Corps. Formally under James Longstreet, and now under Major General Richard Anderson, the First Corps occupied the Confederate right and trailed off to the southeast. The Wilderness fighting had reduced the Confederate army by some 7,750 casualties including Longstreet, one of

Although its manpower reserves were nearly depleted, Robert E. Lee's Army of Northern Virginia was at the peak of its battlefield effectiveness in 1864.

Lee's most brilliant subordinates. who had been accidently shot by his own men in the confusion of the 6 May combat.

Robert E. Lee himself spent 7 May attempting to fathom his opponent's next move through a fog of confusing observations and intelligence reports. Probes and reconnaissance missions revealed a variety of activities taking place throughout the enemy line. Lee's cavalry under Major General Jeb Stuart reported fighting with Federal troopers throughout the morning south of the Army of Northern Virginia and in the afternoon he sent word of battles with Merritt and Gregg near Todd's Tavern. Another report told of wagon trains seen on the move toward Chancellorsville. A reconnaissance by Early's men discovered that the Federal pontoon bridge over the Rapidan at the Germanna Plank Road, had been pulled up and moved, an indication that Grant did not intend to retreat by the path he had entered the Wilderness. Members of Hill's staff also contributed their observations of an artillery park which had limbered up and headed somewhere in the direction of the Federal left. Lee could tell from this that the enemy was preparing a movement, but the nagging question of what his destination might be remained.

Lee could not be absolutely certain of where Grant and Meade were going and for what purpose they were moving. If Grant had given up the fight, he might be attempting to retreat to Fredericksburg. However, he might also be continuing his advance by moving for some point farther south. Lee himself decided it would be wise to operate south of his current position, in the vicinity of Spotsylvania, whatever his enemy was up to. By doing so, he would have the ability to get on the flank of the Federals if they indeed intended to retreat or get in their way if they were actually advancing. In preparation for operations toward Spotsylvania, Stuart received instructions through Lee's assistant adjutant-general, W.H. Taylor, to scout out the roads to the south, in his words to, "follow should the enemy continue his movement toward Spotsylvania Court-House, or should we desire to move on his flank in that direction." In that dispatch, it appeared Lee was leaning toward the belief that the Federals were advancing toward Spotsylvania, "The enemy now and then advance and feel our lines, and the general thinks there is nothing to indicate an intention on his part to retire, but rather that appearances would indicate an intention to move toward Spotsylvania Court-House."

Lee also endeavored to have an infantry force sent to Spotsylvania, requiring a route cut through the Wilderness timber from

Spotsylvania Court House, Virginia, in 1864.

the Plank Road to White Hall Mill, a mission charged to artillery chief Brigadier General William Pendleton and his men. The First Corps, under Richard Anderson, on the right and closest to the destination of the intended movement, was detailed to make the 11-mile march to Spotsylvania starting no later than 0300, moving by Todd's Tavern or Shady Grove Church. Anderson set the time for his march to begin around 2300. Before that appointed hour, Pendleton arrived with the officer who was to act as First Corps' guide for the movement and informed the corps commander that the way was open. Brigadier General Joseph B. Kershaw's division was the first part of Anderson's force to trudge down the rough path followed by Major General Charles Field's men. Stumps and trees not fully removed from the path made the trek tough going for Anderson's tired soldiers, so much so that the new corps commander decided to call a halt for rest after his troops had gone only a mile. Since there was no place suitable for the men to fall out, the forest all around them still being on fire from the Wilderness battle, the command trudged on, reaching Corbin's Bridge at 0100 and then pushed forward to Shady Grove Church where it turned east. Anderson finally halted near dawn just west of the Block House Bridge over the Po River only three miles west of Spotsylvania Court House. Thus while the *Army of the Potomac* was making its way to Spotsylvania Court House, part of the Army of Northern Virginia was also on the move there as well, unknowingly parallelling the march of their adversaries. This coincidence was not so much through the prescience of the leader of the Confederate forces as it was through his good common sense.

As the *Army of the Potomac* and the Army of Northern Virginia left one gruesome battlefield, another one just as terrible lay farther down the road and both sides seemed to be under a spell of misapprehension as their forces advanced toward it. On 8 May at 1000, Assistant Secretary of War Charles Dana, observing the actions of the *Army of the Potomac* for his chief Secretary of War Edwin M. Stanton, wrote back to Washington, "There are no indications that Lee has moved in any direction, and General Grant is decidedly of opinion that he remains in the old place." At about the same time Lee reported to his secretary of war, James A. Seddon, that his enemy was apparently retreating, "The enemy has abandoned his position and is moving toward Fredricksburg." That same day, Lee and Grant would find their enemy at Spotsylvania and begin nearly two weeks of battle.

Robert E. Lee

Robert E. Lee's (1807-1870) military prowess and gentlemanly demeanor made him beloved in the Confederacy, respected in the North, and legendary in the annals of American military history. His legacy of achievement won him the name of "the Gray Fox" and he is recognized as one of the greatest military minds the United States has ever produced.

Lee was descended from significant figures in American history, being the son of Revolutionary War hero Henry "Light Horse" Harry Lee, and related to two signers of the Declaration of Independence. He quickly became quite accomplished himself by graduating from West Point in 1829 second in his class with nearly impeccable grades. His first war service was during Winfield Scott's march on Mexico City during the Mexican War, in which he won three brevets. After the war, he continued to roll up honors including the position of Superintendent of West Point and commander of the 2nd U.S. Cavalry. When John Brown launched his 1859 Virginia raid to spark a slave insurrection, Lee was in command of the force sent to stop him.

As the clouds of Civil War gathered with the secession crisis in 1861, both the North and South sought to convince Lee to join their ranks. The Federal government under Abraham Lincoln offered him the lofty honor of army command, but Lee's allegiance to his native Virginia compelled him to side with the Confederacy. Lee commanded Virginia's state troops before receiving a brigadier general's commission in Confederate service in May, and later the third ranking generalcy in all the Southern armies, being outranked only by Samuel Cooper and Albert S. Johnston. Even if his talent was recognized, it was not effectively used early in the war as he was relegated at first to overseeing the collapsing Confederate hold on West Virginia in August 1861 and then to the supervision of coastal fortifications. Union Major General George Brinton McClellan's offensive up the Virginia Peninsula against the Confederate capital of Richmond provided Lee with the opportunity to burst onto a greater stage and win his undying fame. When Confederate General Joseph Johnston was wounded at the battle of Seven Pines on 31 May 1862, Lee took his place as commander of the Army of Northern Virginia. Late in June, Lee went on to win a smashing set of victories in the Seven Days offensive that turned McClellan's army from the gates of Richmond and forced him to retreat down the Peninsula.

Lee's star was now in ascendence and even greater laurels awaited. After the Peninsula he drove north, winning a signal victory at Second Bull Run (29-30 August 1862) which created the opportunity for his invasion of Maryland. However, Lee's luck was never very good north of the Potomac and unhappy circumstances led him to a defeat at Antietam on 17 September and forced him to retreat to Virginia. There he fended off two Northern offensives, the first under Major General Ambrose Burnside, defeated in a bloody repulse at Fredericksburg on 13 December 1862, and the other being Major General Joseph Hooker's effort, stopped at Chancellorsville on 1-3 May 1863. Lee's masterful division of his smaller army at Chancellorsville to defeat an opponent with much larger numbers has been recognized by many as his greatest battlefield success. Unfortunately, this great victory was only a precursor to one of Lee's worst disasters as a commander.

After Chancellorsvile, Lee took the opportunity to march his army north of the Potomac for a second time, going into southern Pennsylvania where his force encountered the Federal *Army of the Potomac*, now under Major General George G. Meade, outside of Gettysburg. The battle that took place there from 1-3 July was a terrible defeat for the Confederates, one fraught with several costly mistakes, the most infamous being the decision to launch the ill fated charge of George Pickett's division. Over the three days of fighting at Gettysburg, the Army of Northern Virginia lost 28,000 casualties. Lee's still defiant army had no other option but to retreat and on 4 July headed south for Virginia.

In May of 1864, Lee squared off against a new opponent, Lieutenant General Ulysses S. Grant, General in Chief of all the Federal armies, personally on the scene in the East to direct the next offensive of the *Army of the Potomac.* Lee ably parried Grant's moves at the Wilderness (4-5 May 1864), Spotsylvania (7-19 May 1864)

and Cold Harbor (1-3 June 1864), dealing the enemy harsh repulses with significant casualties. But the battles did not stop Grant's advance and the constant Federal offensive denied Lee the opportunity to deliver a counterblow such as those he had used to defeat his previous adversaries. Lee had noted that if his army was driven into a siege near Richmond, defeat would be inevitable. By July, Grant had forced Lee into defensive positions around Petersburg and both armies now waited out the rest of 1864 in the very situation Lee had hoped to avoid.

Lee held out at Petersburg as long as he could, until the deteriorating situation finally forced him to quit his entrenchments on 2 April 1865 and make his way to join General Joseph Johnston's army fighting William T. Sherman's Yankees in North Carolina. Pursuing Union forces cut him off from that route and hounded him to Appomattox Court House where Lee gave in to the inevitable and surrendered on 9 April 1865.

Lee spent his post-war years in relative quiet as president of Washington College, later renamed Washington & Lee University.

There is no doubt that Robert E. Lee's lofty reputation in the record of American military history is deserved. Yet, certainly the "Gray Fox" was not without shortcomings, the most egregious of these being the disaster of Pickett's Charge and his failure to recognize the importance of the Civil War's Western Theater and to fully coordinate operations with fellow generals there. But the fact remains that he did so much with so little, and, almost to the end of the war, he continued to fluster and frighten the adversaries that opposed him by mere reputation alone.

Ulysses S. Grant

When the Civil War broke out, the 39-year-old Ulysses S. Grant (1822-1885) was earning his keep as a mere clerk in his father's store in Galena, Illinois. Only a few years later, he had catapulted from this humble station to the command of all the Federal armies and then a two-term presidency of the United States, a fantastic rise to fame built through Grant's own unyielding determination, his stewardship by political officials, and luck.

Grant, originally named Hiram Ulysses Grant, called Ulysses by his family, entered the United States Military Academy at West Point thanks to his father's urging and influence with a Senator from the Grants' home state Ohio. The young Grant was at first daunted by the possibility of going to the Academy, fearing he did not have the capabilities to endure the "acquirements" necessary to succeed there. However his concerns proved all for naught and he graduated, though as an unexceptional 21st in his class of 39 students, to attain a commission in the infantry. Grant also left the Academy with a formal change to his name as well. The letter of recommendation from his Congressman which had gotten him into West Point listed the new cadet as U.S. Grant instead of H.U. Grant. Grant evidently approved of the change and stuck with Ulysses as his first name.

Grant saw action in the Mexican War, winning two brevets and serving in the legendary campaigns of both Winfield Scott and Zachary Taylor. The laurels temporarily ended there: Grant resigned his commission as a captain in 1854, the same day he obtained it, and tried to find success in civilian life as a farmer and rent collector before taking a position at his father's store.

When the war broke out, Grant returned to military affairs, at first not finding much interest or use for his services. Still, he slowly began to rise through the ranks, becoming first a colonel in the *21st Illinois* in June 1861, obtaining a brigadier general's commission on 4 August through the help of his political sponsor Congressman Elihu Washburne, and then commander of the *Department of Southeast Illinois*. In November of 1861, he boldly attacked a Confederate force at Belmont, Missouri, losing the battle, but impressing his superiors. The next year, he led a successful offensive against the Confederate forts

Henry and Donelson, winning the nickname "Unconditional Surrender" as a result of the terms he offered Fort Donelson's defenders. After this success, Grant narrowly avoided disaster through his trademark tenacity and clear thinking when his army was surprised at the battle of Shiloh (6-7 April 1862).

Grant spent most of the next year engaged in attempts to seize the Mississippi river town of Vicksburg. Many different plans and schemes were employed to take the key city, each one flustered by the Confederates or through natural and logistical difficulties. Despite a number of failures, Lincoln stood by Grant, saying, "I can't spare this man, he fights." In April of 1863, Grant gambled boldly by cutting his communications to assault Vicksburg from the south. The scheme worked so well that he defeated Confederate forces under General Joseph Johnston and Lieutenant General John Pemberton, driving the latter into Vicksburg which was put under siege. On 4 July 1863, Pemberton surrendered the town and his 20,000 troops.

Vicksburg led to the promotion of Grant to commander of the *Military Division of the Mississippi*, consisting of the combined military departments west of the Appalachians and east of the Mississippi River. In this position, Grant led the *Army of the Cumberland* and the *Army of the Tennessee* in the victories over Braxton Bragg's Army of Tennessee at the battles of Chattanooga from 23-25 November 1863. Grant's continued record of accomplishment led to further promotion as well as a trip East.

In March of 1864, Grant was appointed to the restored rank of lieutenant general, only previously held by George Washington. More importantly, he was now general in chief and could direct all the National armies toward delivering a death blow to the Confederacy. Grant's plan toward this goal was a simple one, to engage in a series of coordinated offensives to subdue the enemy, the primary elements being an offensive by George G. Meade with the *Army of the Potomac* in the East and one by armies under William T. Sherman in the West. While claiming to give Meade a free hand, Grant exerted control over the movements of the *Army of the Potomac* and played a leading role in many of the battles that took place during that army's march south beginning in May of 1864. By June of 1864, Grant had driven his opponent, General Robert E. Lee, commanding the Army of Northern Virginia, back to Petersburg and pinned him down in a siege that lasted into the spring of 1865. On 2 April the Army of Northern Virginia would begin its last march, pursued by Grant's forces. The chase ended at Appomattox Court House with Lee's surrender on 9 April. The contrast between Lee and Grant during the signing of surrender terms was striking. The Confederate general stood tall, buttoned to the collar in a splendid new uniform with sword and sash. Grant, who had not expected the surrender, was slightly stooped and dressed in his mud spattered "traveling clothes," the outfit of a private with his lieutenant general's straps pinned to it. Grant offered generous terms to his adversary including paroles for the captured troops and permission for them to keep their private property. At Lee's request, Grant authorized Federal commissaries to give rations to the hungry Southern soldiers. Lee's surrender was the harbinger of the final end of the war, and over the next few months, the rest of the Confederate forces in the field capitulated.

Ending the Civil War as the Union's foremost military hero, Grant made a perfect presidential candidate and was unanimously nominated by the Republican Convention to be that party's candidate in 1868. Grant defeated his opponent, former governor of New York Horatio Seymour, by winning most of the electoral votes, but only by a narrow margin of popular votes. The warrior served two inglorious terms as president with an administration plagued by scandals and the corrup-

tion of his subordinates. After his service in politics, Grant enjoyed a more happy life by traveling the world, returning home only to suffer from huge business losses and failing health. Fortunately, the composition of his memoirs and articles on his battles, aided by an admiring Samuel Clemens, provided a source of income for his family. He died on 25 July 1885.

Perhaps Grant's greatest trait as a commander during the Civil War was his unyielding tenacity. During his overland Virginia campaign of 1864, few of the battles that were fought under his direction could be called victories. Yet, it was his determination to never turn back and keep constantly in movement that forced his superlative foe, Lee, to keep on the defensive and match Federal moves. This, together with his plan of simultaneous advances on all fronts, slowly ground the South down and allowed the Republic to be united once again.

Spotsylvania

The Civil War took many little-known localities and obscure landmarks across the American landscape and attached to them a significance that would reverberate throughout the history of the United States. In few cases was this more true than the area known as Spotsylvania.

Spotsylvania Court House was a

hamlet on the southeast corner of the scrubby woodland known as the Wilderness. Its size and obscurity belied its strategic importance for both armies. Roads radiated from the town in several directions, most importantly south to Richmond and northeast to Fredericksburg. It was also a point on stagecoach and telegraph routes and nearby was the rail artery of the Richmond and Fredericksburg Railroad.

While Spotsylvania's landscape was more open than the thick growth of the Wilderness, other natural characteristics made the ground unsuitable for an offensive campaign. Four thin waterways ran through the area from east to west, called (from south to north) the Mat, Ta, Po and Ny, with all of these eventually joining into the Mattapony River. Spotsylvania lay between the Ma and Po, two comparatively small streams with steep banks sometimes sided by marshes. The landscape between the streams alternated between clearings and dense growths of hazel, pine, and scrub oak.

This sylvan scene also had signs of human habitation as numerous farms dotted the landscape, occupied by the hearty stock of people that tried to carve a rough living out of the inhospitable terrain. Many of these places, such as McCoull's, Landrum's, and Myer's farms, would lend their names to battlefield sites where thousands of men would engage in life and death struggles.

CHAPTER II

Laurel Hill

8 May 1864

On 8 May, the battles around Spotsylvania began, as both armies gravitated down the maze of northern Virginia tracks and routes for that tiny crossroads town. Fighting began in the early morning hours of 8 May as Sheridan's cavalry continued the previous day's mission of pushing the enemy's troopers south. Merritt's cavalry was finally on the move down the Brock Road around 0330 and found elements of Fitzhugh Lee's command blocking his path. A running fight developed in the morning gloom with troopers exchanging shots at the crackling flame licks of carbines. The Confederates were slowly pushed back. In their wake, the Federals found obstacles of cut trees laid across the road. Nearby were enemy troops ready to fire on any who ventured forward to move them. Around 0500, Wilson's cavalry had moved out from Alrich's and on to the Fredericksburg Road, getting into a fight with Thomas Rosser's cavalry brigade near Spotsylvania Court House.

Merritt's slow progress clearing away the enemy compelled him to call upon Warren's *V Corps* for aid at 0600. Warren got his corps moving with Robinson's division in the advance. The march would be hard going, the day was going to be intensely hot and the men were already exhausted from the exertions of

A Union hospital was set up at Alsop's farm during the Spotsylvania campaign.

the previous night. Combined with weather and weariness was the fact that the terrain the *V Corps* would cross would not prove at all expedient for infantry movements, a point Warren himself noted, "It is difficult to do much with troops in an expeditious manner in these dense woods." Still, the Confederate cavalry, now reinforced by a four-gun battery was slowly forced back by Warren's troops. At 0800 the Federals were only three miles from Spotsylvania at a clearing near Alsop's farm close to the intersection of the Brock Road with the Old Court House Road. Across the some 400 yards of open ground was a low rise called Laurel Hill where Fitzhugh Lee's Confederate troopers were busily digging in preparation for making a stand.

Lee's men would not be fighting on their own. Confederate infantrymen of Anderson's First Corps had been on the move during the early morning of the eighth as well, reaching Old Court House between 0700 and 0800. The corps' new commander was aware of the situation at Laurel Hill as a couple of couriers had arrived hurriedly informing him that Fitz Lee's troopers were hard pressed and desperately needed help. The first courier encountered Major John C. Haskell's artillery brigade. Haskell knew the messenger and was able to get a look at the dispatch, word from Jeb Stuart himself asking that reinforcements be sent to the action taking place on the Brock Road. Realizing the gravity of the situation, the quick-thinking Haskell sent his friend on to find Anderson while he immediately took his own command into the battle. When Anderson received the courier's missive, he found himself facing a painful dilemma; his objective set by Lee was to take Spotsylvania Court House, a mission that would conflict with sending in troops to help out the beleaguered Fitz Lee. When another courier reached Anderson at Old Court House with news of the beleaguered cavalry, the corps commander acted decisively by ordering Kershaw to send two of his brigades to help the troopers fighting on the Brock Road. Kershaw sent in his own former brigade of South Carolinians under Colonel John W. Henagan and Brigadier General Benjamin G. Humphreys' Mississippians. These marched northwards for nearly a mile when they met a trooper urging them to quickly make for a breastwork of rails before the Federals got there. The troops rushed forward to the works on a hill near the Old Court House Road and Brock Road intersection, directed to their positions by Stuart himself. Haskell's guns were already there directing their fire towards the oncoming enemy.

Fitz Lee was also encountering difficulty holding off the Federal troopers of Wilson's cavalry division moving toward Spotsylvania down the Fredericksburg Road from the northeast. A courier brought word to Anderson that a mere cavalry regiment was all there was to hold off this Yankee threat and these outnumbered Confederates could not hold out for long. Two brigades under Wofford and Bryan were sent there to help. The threat they were sent to counter was potentially critical, for Wilson's cavalry had actually come very close to taking the Federal objective of Spotsylvania. His troopers had driven the

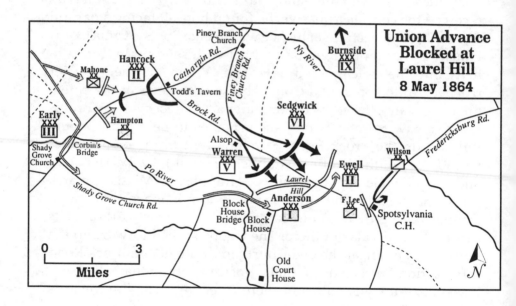

Brigadier General John C. Robinson, wounded while attempting to clear Laurel Hill on the approach to Spotsylvania.

enemy from the town and they were preparing to hold it against the new threat of the approaching Confederate infantry. The impact of Wilson's seizure of the town became a historical what-if when an order from Sheridan forced the Union cavalry commander to retire.

Meanwhile, at around 0830, the *V Corps* infantry was massing for the attack on Laurel Hill. Warren had the right man on the scene to drive an attack home, Brigadier General John Cleveland Robinson, a veteran commander who had been in some hot spots as a brigade commander in the Peninsula campaign, Second Bull Run and Fredericksburg. He had assumed division command at Chancellorsville and with 2,500 men had fought off twice that number at Gettysburg. His assessment of the situation before Laurel Hill was that the dominating position of the rise over the Brock Road had to be taken if he was continue his

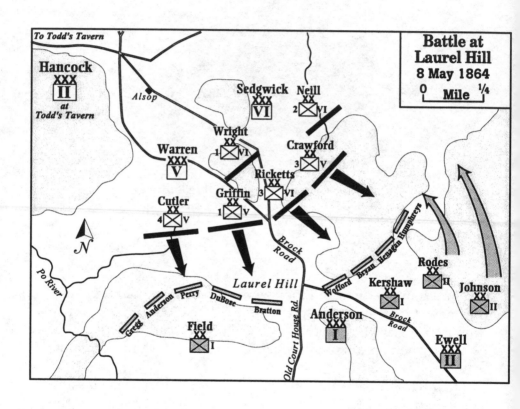

advance to Spotsylvania Court House. All he lacked was the men to do it and the time to get them. Corps commander Warren urged Robinson to press on, to which the division commander replied he would need his entire division to be successful and an attack would have to wait until it was brought up. He only had his lead force, Colonel Peter Lyle's weary *First Brigade*, on hand and this desperately needed to rest after its exertions throughout the morning. Warren at first allowed Robinson time to rest his men, a needed pause that was cut short after 10 minutes. The impatient Warren now peremptorily ordered Robinson to attack with the forces he had. The division commander reluctantly obeyed by sending in Lyle's brigade and the *4th Maryland Regiment* that had come up from Colonel Andrew Denison's *Third Brigade*, also known as the *Maryland Brigade*.

Lyle's command of regiments from Maine, Massachusetts, New York and Pennsylvania advanced to tackle the 400 yards of ground before the enemy position, supposedly held only by Confederate cavalrymen. Blasts of musket fire from the 2nd and 3rd South Carolina Regiments of Henegan's brigade informed the Yankees that they were mistaken, the infantry of the Army of Northern Virginia was on the scene as well. Already disorganized from the broken ground they were attempting to cross, most of Lyle's brigade fell back quickly in retreat while the more stalwart managed to reach the base of the hill where they found cover to rest and dig in.

The rest of Robinson's division, Richard Coulter's *Second Brigade* and Denison's *Maryland Brigade*, was then committed to the attack. Warren himself was on hand to impress the men with the importance of their mission, calling out, "Never mind cannon! Never mind bullets! Press on and clear this road! It's the only way to get your rations!" Robinson decided to press his troops by taking part in the assault himself. He cheered his men as they drove within 50 yards of the Confederate line where a musket ball mangled his left knee. The ghastly wound forced him to be removed from the field and required the amputation of his leg. Robinson's fall led to the demise of the entire attack as Richard Coulter wrote later in his official report, "His being

The eyewitness sketch of Warren rallying troops at Laurel Hill catches the desperation of the moment.

disabled at this juncture was a severe blow to the division and certainly influenced the fortunes of the day. The want of our commanding officer prevented that concert of action which alone could have overcome the enemy in the front." Robinson wasn't the only high ranking officer to be disabled during the fighting, *Maryland Brigade* commander Denison fell as well with a wound that would also cost him a limb. The only Federals to keep a toehold on Laurel Hill were those elements of Lyle's command at the base of the rise, and these were driven to the rear by the arrival of Humphreys' Mississippi regiments. Captain Kinsley of the *39th Massachusetts* from Lyle's Brigade was in tears at the sight of his company after its engagement in the fight, crying out, "Look at my company! Only seven men left out of eighty-seven!" He was consoled that many men were lost in

In the finished version of the drawing of Warren at Laurel Hill that appeared in Northern newspapers, the general has become more calm and his troops more resolute.

nearby woods and indeed many did return. Still, Robinson's division had been crippled by the fruitless assaults of the day.

Warren was not yet willing to give up his attempts to take the hill. He had two more divisions to commit and these were being brought up before the Confederate position. Griffin's division launched its attack with the *Third Brigade*, under First Bull Run hero Brigadier General Joseph Jackson Bartlett, in the lead. These men were not in any condition to drive a successful attack home, most being tired and hungry from the morning's march in the hot sun. They were not even allowed the opportunity to take a brief rest before being committed to the attack. Federal commanders were still under the misapprehension that they were only facing an enemy cavalry force that could easily be brushed aside and an assault should be made quickly. An enthusiastic aide to Bartlett displayed this ignorance as he rode by to encourage the men while they were forming, shouting,

Hancock's troops guard Todd's Tavern on May 8. Protective barricades are now being built even for temporary halts.

"Hurry up, or you won't get a shot at them!" The concerned Lieutenant Colonel Connor of the *44th New York* sent an aide to Bartlett asking for permission to at least have the men stack their backpacks before going into battle. The brigadier responded, "No, tell Colonel Connor their is no force in our front but cavalrymen...." His troops would pay dearly as a result of this mistaken belief.

The Federals discovered their error soon after their assault began. The musketry they experienced was called "murderous" and Eugene Nash of the *44th New York* bitterly recalled, "The idea that the position was held only by cavalry was soon exploded." The troops continued onward and Bartlett's men were able to get near enough to the enemy line for close combat, at one point getting so near to the enemy's lines that an officer of the *44th New York* emptied his pistol into the Confederate ranks with telling effect and soldiers of the *83rd Pennsylvania* were able to use their bayonets "freely over the enemy's works." The Yankees did not stand for long; a Confederate force appeared on their left flank and compelled the Yankees to retire. The historian of the *44th New York* recalled of his regiment's desperate situation at the time, "It became apparent to all that the only movement by which the Forty Fourth could be saved from capture or destruction, was to break for the rear and make a hasty retreat. The line quickly dissolved, some to escape, some to fall and some to be captured." The retreating brigade ran into the rest of Griffin's command trying to advance and all fell back to the rear. The Confederates offered a pursuit, but were checked.

The arrival of the *Fourth Division* under Brigadier General Lysander Cutler gave Warren one more opportunity to renew the attack. These tired troops managed to get a momentary rest before they too contributed in the fighting. Soldiers of the *Iron Brigade* of Western troops had begun to boil coffee when orders came to advance forcing some to have their drinks "on the run." Cutler's command advanced in good order for some 250 yards before the enemy unleashed a "brisk fire" that brought it to a halt. Then Confederates appeared on its right, driving it back in confusion. Colonel Edward S. Bragg, who led Cutler's *Third Brigade*, wrote of the impact on his brigade of the Confederate blows, "...the lines upon the right and left gave way and a panic ensued, which for a moment threatened a total demoralization of the command."

Just as Warren's troops had been arriving on the field, so were the rest of Anderson's Confederate First Corps units. Major General Charles Field's division, formerly John Bell Hood's, had arrived during the fight and some his regiments were dispatched to areas of need during the *V Corps* attacks. His final position was on the left of Henegan's position thus extending the growing Confederate line to the Po River. More Confederates were on the way. Around 0800, Lee had ordered Ewell's Second Corps, Major General Robert E. Rodes' division in the lead, to march south past Parker's Store, eventually taking up the Catharpin Road to Shady Grove Church. The march would be the longest of any of Lee's corps and the trip a difficult one

Major General John Sedgwick was to become the most famous casualty of the Spotsylvania campaign.

thanks to the thick dust from the roads and smoke from the burning woods.

The rest of the *Army of the Potomac* was converging on the scene as well. Warren informed his superiors at 1230 that he was blocked by infantry from Longstreet's corps, was low on ammunition and would be unable to press on unless he received more reinforcements. Grant, at Piney Branch Church when he received the news, was eager for the opportunity to crush the enemy force before the rest of the Confederate army moved to join it. He ordered Sedgwick's *VI Corps* to Warren's position in the hopes that a combined attack of both their corps might yield success. The *II* and *IX Corps* were also directed to march in the direction of the fighting to support Warren.

Just as an unknown race had developed between Anderson and Warren, so another race developed between Ewell and

Sedgwick. Sedgwick's lead units reached the field around 1030, but it wasn't until 1700 that his entire command was up to join in the fighting, a tardiness Grant believed must have been unavoidable since in his words, "he [Sedgwick] was never at fault when serious work was to be done...." Yet, Sedgwick's delay had allowed Ewell's troops to arrive and take position on the right of Anderson's Corps to the east of the Brock Road. Grant's hope of attacking Anderson's command while it was still isolated had evaporated. However, an attack was still going to be made.

When the Federal combined attack got underway at 1800, it was one that Meade's chief of staff Andrew Humphreys called "partial, and not too determined and vigorous." Warren's troops were too tired from marching and battle and Sedgwick's men were too unfamiliar with the situation there for any coordinated effort to take place. Probably less than half the troops designated to make the attack actually stepped forward. The *Third* and *Fourth Brigade*s of Brigadier General Thomas Neill's *Second Division* of the *VI Corps* and Brigadier General Samuel Crawford's *Pennsylvania Reserve Division* stumbled upon Rodes' Division going into position. The Federals were forced back by determined attacks by Brigadier General Cullen A. Battle's and Brigadier General Stephen D. Ramseur's Brigades in combat that was sometimes as close as hand-to-hand. The growing evening brought an end to the fighting, forcing Rodes' Confederates to give up their counterattack as darkness descended, withdrawing to their main line under cover of darkness.

The battle of Laurel Hill was a grave disappointment for the Union. Though getting a move ahead of the Confederate army, mistakes and delays had hindered the progress of the *Army of the Potomac*, allowing Anderson to reach Spotsylvania Court House to impede its advance. Uncoordinated attacks then failed to drive him away before the rest of the Confederate army could arrive and over 1,500 men had been lost in the day's failed efforts. There was much bitterness over the attack in the ranks of the Federal troops who had fought at Laurel Hill on 8 May. One skirmisher grumbled, "pretty dismounted cavalry carrying knapsacks." Nash of the *44th New York* wrote, "A feeling prevailed that proper foresight had not been exercised in ordering an inadequate force to make the charge." Lieutenant Colonel Dewitt C. McCoy wrote of the losses of his *83rd Pennsylvania* at Laurel Hill, "There we lost many of our best and bravest men."

Charge!
Great Charges During the Civil War

The Civil War has often been called the first modern war, since it had the trappings of the brutal combat that would become the grim reputation of 20th Century conflicts. Like the wars in the next century, particularly World War I, Civil War soldiers had a considerable reliance on defensive fortifications and used repeating breech loading firearms, wire communications, ironclad fighting vessels and so on. However, others have termed the conflict the last of the Napoleonic age since battle tactics were primarily the same as used in the European wars in the early 19th Century and whatever innovations that were employed during the Civil War had no real impact on the way the conflict was being waged. While, indeed, tactics had not changed much since those used on fields like Waterloo, a revolution had taken place in Civil War combat that served as a portent for the way fighting would be waged in the future. Never was this more evident, perhaps, than during the battle of Spotsylvania.

The reason a change in tactics was necessary during the Civil War period was the development of the rifle. Previously, armies relied on the musket, a smoothbore muzzle loading weapon with an effective range of around 100 yards. The relative inaccuracy of the weapon meant it was only effective if troops were bunched together in lines of men who could then fire a volley.

Furthermore, the low range gave the attacker an advantage, since he could close on an enemy position with little chance of getting hit, only suffering severely when he was almost upon his prey. By then, the clumsy slow-loading musket could get at best only a couple of shots off before the fighting became hand-to-hand. The rifled musket with grooves inside the barrel which allowed a soldier to deliver a load accurately and at longer ranges was available in Napoleonic times, but required the bullet be forced down the muzzle, because of the grooves needed to speed its flight, a lengthy process that rendered it inadequate to the needs of most combat troops.

Before the mid-19th Century, French officers Captain Henri Gustave Delvigne and Captain Claude-Etienne Minie made the rifle a more usable weapon when they developed a bullet that could be easily loaded down a rifle without the force required for the earlier variety. This device had a hollow base which allowed it to expand from the gases resulting from the fired gunpowder. The bullet then took the rifled groves of the barrel that would give it greater accuracy over longer distances. Now the infantry had a weapon that could fire accurately over two to three times the capability of the musket. They could even begin firing with an effect at a range of 500 yards, with the ability of delivering 10 volleys before the attacker could respond with effect. This fact led to what one historian called a domination of the bullet over the battlefield. With the infantry armed with a rifle under the protective cover of fortifications, charging infantry attackers would suffer mercilessly before they had time to apply the shock of their charge; cavalry charges would be all but useless against such firepower; and artillery would have to be pulled back from the lines of battle to escape from being victim to enemy fusillades, thus diminishing their effectiveness. The entire nature of warfare had changed.

Regrettably, many Civil War commanders were slow to realize it. Though the rifle had been issued by the United States in 1855 and was used in great quantities by both sides, tactics had not been changed to adapt to the new situation. Both sides then offered up their forces to each other in parallel lines to slug it out or charged across lengthy fields of open ground to attack an enemy position. Charges against fortified positions yielded the worst results with attackers suffering severely: Ambrose Burnside suffered 13,000 casualties while inflicting 5,000 on Lee at Fredericksburg on 13 May and Grant's May 22 attack at Vicksburg cost 3,200 men to 500 Confederates. The most infamous such catastrophe was Pickett's Charge at Gettysburg on 3 July 1863 where nearly half the attacking force of 13,000 men was lost.

However, while the proper development of offensive tactics was not taking place, there were innovations in defensive methods. Troops were increasingly learning the importance of fortifications for their safety and their ability to repel an attack. By 1864, whenever an army stopped in preparation for battle, soldiers began to dig in in preparation for the fighting. These trenches could be quite extensive with traverses and dirt parapets strengthened by logs, giving extensive cover. In front lay cleared fields of fire, to make any attacker an open target, and a dense network of abatis laid out to break up any assaults. Once properly built, a good network of fortifications, allowing troops to fire and load as well as to receive ammunition and reinforcements without much exposure to enemy shots, was almost impregnable.

It wasn't until the battles at Spotsylvania that a new innovation in offensive tactics was employed which won a significant result. The leading mind behind the innovation was a young infantry colonel, Emory Upton. Upton's idea was to attack with a narrow column of a large number of troops which could break through enemy works by its sheer weight. To succeed, this column would have to make a surprise attack close to the enemy lines. Fortunately for Upton, he had an excellent opportunity to test his theory on 10 May 1864 when a path through a wood was found that would enable his assaulting column to get within 200 yards of the enemy position. The attack was a temporary success, netting up to 1,200 Confederate prisoners. Further opportunities were lost when attacks to support Upton never material- ized. The following Union attack on the Confederate line at Spotsylvania was modeled on Upton's attack and while successful, showed the defect in such an assault. Once attacking forces managed to break through their enemy's fortifications, the as- saulting columns deteriorated into confusion. This then allowed a de- fender to deliver an organized coun- terblow against their flustered oppo- nent, such as Lee and his army was able to do on 12 May 1864.

Despite Upton's innovation, both armies continued to rely on attacks over open ground by lines of troops. Continually this led to costly re- sults, such as the loss of 7,000 Union troops in a disastrous attack on Cold Harbor on 30 June 1864 and 6,000 Confederates in John Bell Hood's ill-fated assault on 30 No- vember 1864 at Franklin. Mean- while, fortifications became the sta- ple of most battlefields as cam- paigns in the East and West stale- mated into sieges.

Whatever the failure or success during the Civil War in adopting new battlefield techniques on the bullet-dominated battlefield, pain- ful lessons had been learned that could have saved the lives of thou- sands of European soldiers during World War I. However, staffs and commanders on the other side of the Atlantic viewed the Civil War as something peculiar to America and not worthy of much study. When World WarII lapsed into a bloody stalemate because of the power of the bullet, increased by the use of the machine gun, European armies would take cover behind trenches similar to those used before Peters- burg and Atlanta.

CHAPTER III

Maneuvering for Position

8-9 May

As one battle at Spotsylvania came to an end, both armies were converging their remaining forces on the fields, farms and woods north of the town. Lee's forces would arrive to spend the next two days entrenching a formidable set of fortifications while Grant would seek a weakness in his enemy's position to exploit. The new situation allowed a musical pun to be played on Grant. After the lieutenant general and his staff set up their headquarters at Piney Branch Church, a marching band caught sight of him and struck up a tune. Grant's subordinates broke into laughter, confusing the General who asked what all the fun was about. "Why," one of his officers replied, "they are playing 'Ain't I glad to get out ob de wilderness.'"

This amusement was soon overshadowed by a intense clash of tempers between two of the leading commander in the *Army of the Potomac*. Sheridan's handling of the entire *Army of the Potomac*'s cavalry throughout the movement fueled an intense bitter anger in George Gordon Meade and he intended to give the diminutive commander a dressing down. When Sheridan arrived at Meade's headquarters at Piney Branch Church between 1100 and 1200 on 8 May, Meade blasted him with charges of blundering, making improper dispositions and allowing his

The **Army of the Potomac** *crossing the River Ny.*

cavalry to block the road the day before. As Horace Porter described the scene, "Meade was possessed of an excitable temper which under irritating circumstances became almost ungovernable. He had worked himself into a towering passion regarding the delays encountered in the forward movement, and when Sheridan appeared went at him with hammer and tongs, accusing him of blunders, and charging him with not making a proper disposition of troops, and letting the cavalry block the advance of the infantry." Sheridan had not only of an equal fierceness to Meade's, but, according to Porter, "all the hotspur in his nature was aroused." He launched into a retort, spiced with a variety of expletives, that Meade had countermanded his orders, exposed his troops to unnecessary dangers, and hampered his movements. He further stated that if he could concentrate all the cavalry, he would take the entire force against Jeb Stuart and whip him. An infuriated Meade reported the entire incident to Grant. The composed lieutenant general practically ignored Sheridan's insubordination to focus on the bold claim about beating Stuart and responded nonchalantly, "Did Sheridan say that? Well, he generally knows what he is talking about. Let him start right out and do it." By 1300 on 8 May, Sheridan had orders to fulfill his boast.

While the Union cavalry began to take off on its grand raid, the infantry of the *IX* and *II Corps* were heading south toward Spotsylvania. The *IX Corps* was moving in on the town from the northeast, aiming for an enigmatic place listed on a map merely as "Gate," supposedly four miles from Spotsylvania Court House. No one was ever sure what "Gate" might have been or if it even existed, for it was never found anywhere outside of a map. Burnside got his march started around 0300 on 9 May moving a short distance down the Orange Plank Road before running into Sheridan's cavalry preparing for their raid and was forced to wait for an hour for the roads to clear. The *IX Corps* then spent most of the early morning moving southeast to the Fredericksburg Road where it turned southwest, arriving near the Gayle house before 0715, close to where the road crossed the Ny River. Burnside's lead division, Brigadier General Orlando Willcox's, began to cross the Ny at 0900 getting into a skirmish with Confederate troops on the other side of the stream. Willcox, a division commander with the *IX Corps* since 1862, became more frantic as his troops engaged an enemy, possibly in numbers larger than his own force. At 1145, he sent an excited message to Burnside, "The contest extremely doubtful. Enemy have developed themselves equal, or vastly superior in numbers, to mine. Have been driven in at some points, but have recovered for the most part. Hill's and Longstreet's corps are reported at Spotsylvania. You cannot have received my dispatches. I am heavily engaged against superior numbers. Where is Stevenson." At 1200, no doubt to Willcox's relief, Brigadier General Thomas Stevenson's division began to cross and took its place on his right and to the northeast of the rest of the *Army of the Potomac*. Willcox reported the fighting in his front had tapered off around the time of Stevenson's arrival though he felt the situation was still questionable if the enemy attacked with heavier reinforcements. While Willcox worried, Burnside received orders from Grant at 0845 requesting him to find routes leading from his current position to the *Army of the Potomac*.

Concern over the *IX Corps'* connection with the rest of the army would remain a major difficulty in the days to come.

Hancock's troops were heading toward the opposite side of the field from the *IX Corps* on 9 May, bearing down on Spotsylvania from the northwest, encountering enemy forces as they came. Hancock's *II Corps* had reached Todd's Tavern the day before where they relieved Gregg's cavalry and set about entrenching. Nearby Confederates proved belligerent, leading to some small fighting. The *140th Pennsylvania* of the *First Division, First Brigade* got embroiled in a skirmish after they had been issued a ration of crackers, an affair the soldiers later named the "Cracker Fight." The morning of 9 May, Hancock reported that the enemy was moving in on his position though, this time, no force bent on aggression materialized. Orders then came for Hancock's force to join the rest of the army to the south while leaving a division and some artillery at Todd's Tavern. The *II Corps* set out down the Brock Road that afternoon, eventually forming on Warren's right and entrenching on high ground overlooking the Po River and the Shady Grove Church Road to the south of it. Later in the day, Brigadier Gershom Mott's *Fourth Division* of Hancock's command would be ordered to take position on Sedgwick's left, in between the *VI* and *IX Corps* and was underway at 0300 on the morning of 10 May.

While the *II* and *IX Corps* moved up to the area outside of Spotsylvania, the *V* and *VI Corps* dug in, preparing and strengthening their entrenchments. Meade's unhappiness with Warren's handling of the Laurel Hill debacle led him to make Sedgwick the overall commander of both *V* and the *VI Corps*. The unimpressed Sedgwick allowed Warren to attend to his own affairs as if the order had never been issued, later telling Warren's aid Washington Roebling, "...just tell General Warren to go on and command his own corps as usual. I have perfect confidence that he will do what is right, and knows what to do with his corps."

The Federal army planned no aggressive operations on the ninth, allowing troops to dig trenches and commands to readjust their lines. Angry shots were occasionally fired from sharp-

Random sniping on May 9 cost the life of General Sedgwick. Nearby was this hastily erected "fire proof" where he declined to take cover.

shooters on both sides, actively peppering their adversaries with deadly missives. For some star-crossed reason, the day's desultory fire proved particularly costly for the Union high command with two generals falling to snipers' bullets. On the morning of the ninth, Uncle John Sedgwick had been in Porter's words particularly "cheerful and hopeful" and "the picture of buoyant life and health." He was in a playful mood and spent the morning supervising his lines with a jubilant and joking manner. His close proximity to the skirmish lines and disrespect for the danger posed by enemy sharpshooters put him at unneccessary risk. While remonstrating a soldier for dodging Confederate bullets, one such bullet hit him in the face, delivering a mortal wound. The gallant Sedgwick spun to the ground dying. Grant was considerably disheartened by the news of Sedgwick's death. When told, the stunned general twice asked,

Sedgwick was fatally stricken while standing near these two cannon. The scene was almost totally unchanged when his monument was erected 24 years later.

"Is he really dead?" After being assured that the news was true, the lieutenant general sadly noted the importance of Sedgwick's fall, "His loss to this army is greater than the loss of a whole division of troops." To the ranks of the *VI Corps*, Sedgwick's death meant more than the loss of their commander. Soldier Henry George wrote, "To our men the death of 'Uncle John' as he was called, seemed an awful disaster. He had commanded the corps so long and so well, that his men had... come to regard him as a sort of father to the Sixth Corps, and his death shocked them with a feeling of bereavement, much as the death of a parent would have done." Command of the *VI Corps* now fell to Horatio G. Wright, a competent officer who had commanded a division in the corps since May 1863. The day after Sedgwick's death, the commander of the *IX Corps' First Division*, Brigadier General Thomas G. Stevenson, also fell with a mortal wound when the back of his head was pierced by a lethal bullet while

Horatio G. Wright, prominent at Spotsyl-
vania, was typical of the numerous compe-
tent officers rising through the ranks of the
Union army, while Confederate ranks were
thinning.

he was talking with his staff. Corps commander Burnside later
said that he was "pained beyond measure" by Stevenson's loss.
For the time being, Burnside did not have an officer of equal
rank to replace the fallen brigadier and a mere colonel, David
Leasure of the *Second Brigade*, took command of the entire *First
Division*.

While the Federals settled, Lee drew the last of his forces to
the Confederate line at Spotsylvania where his army dug a
position that would dramatically influence the sanguinary
events of the days to come. Early was away from the rest of the
army at Shady Grove with the Third Corps on the morning of
the ninth when he received orders to move down the Shady
Grove Church Road towards Spotsylvania. His troops were on

the march at 0600 and went into position to the right of Ewell, covering the approach to Spotsylvania from Fredericksburg.

The Confederates constructed a five to seven mile line laid out by Lee's chief engineer Martin Smith who attempted to fix both flanks of the army on the banks of the Po River while using the defensive aspects of the local terrain to full advantage, following an arcing ridge and passing through scrubby and dense woods. From the Po bending northeast was Anderson's Corps holding the left in a line about one-and-a-quarter miles long. Field's Division was laid out on the left heading almost west on the high ground before the Shady Grove Bridge Road with John Gregg's Brigade on the very left followed by Anderson's and Law's Brigades, Benning's Brigade under Colonel Dudley M. Dubose, and Jenkin's Brigade under Colonel John Bratton. The division then joined with Kershaw's at the Brock Road where Wofford's Brigade swung up to the northeast with Bryan's, Kershaw's under Colonel John W. Henagan and Humphrey's Brigades. Humphreys command connected to the left of the Second Corps which veered sharply almost due north for nearly a half mile, with Ramseur's and Daniel's Brigades of Rodes' Division. The leftmost brigade of Rodes' Division under Brigadier General George Doles along with Walker's, Hays', and Witcher's Brigades and Steuart's of Johnson's Division bent the line back to the northeast on high open ground and then almost due east for 400 yards and then after another angle turned almost directly southward for 600 or 700 yards. The Confederate line began trailing off to the southeast with the Third Corps holding this position past the Fredericksburg Road with its divisions.

The Confederate position bulged out with a salient nearly three quarters of a mile long and almost 1,200 yards at its widest point, a huge spearhead pointing almost directly north. This oddity existed so as to allow Ewell's troops to hold the high ground at the salient's apex, ground which if in the hands of the Federals would allow them an artillery position commanding the Confederate line. The Southerners fortified their line with grim professionalism, using whatever tools might prove handy.

Confederate entrenchments near the "Bloody Angle" salient at Spotsylvania, an example of what the men of the Army of Northern Virginia could accomplish in a short time with primitive tools.

Frank Mixson's unit, Company E of the 1st South Carolina, had gotten to work soon after the fighting stopped on 8 May, "the men, of their own accord, commenced to cut down pine trees to build breastworks. The only tools we had for this purpose were the little hand axes, about three inches wide, which some of the men had. These they carried in their belts and used them to chop wood for fires. But now they put them to bigger use and would not hesitate to jump onto a pine tree that would square twenty inches; and it was surprising how soon they would have it down, cut off, trimmed up and cut off again." Strong defenses were constructed with abatis thrown out in front and mounds of fence rails covered with dirt protecting the trenches. With troops well sheltered from enemy fire behind these constructions and their musketry bolstered with cannon strategically placed about their position, the Confederate line at Spotsylvania would prove nearly impregnable against traditional infantry attacks. The *Army of the Potomac*'s chief of staff, Andrew Humphreys, noted the work of his adversaries with grim admiration, "With such intrenchments as these, having artillery throughout, with flank fire along their lines whenever practicable, with the rifled

Grant reconnoitering before the Confederate entrenchments at Spotsylvania, from an eyewitness sketch.

While the Spotsylvania campaign was under way, Benjamin But-ler's Union army had landed closer to Richmond and secured Dre-wry's Bluff, whose formidable heights can be seen here from the James River.

muskets then in use, which were as effective at three hundred yards as the smooth-bore muskets at sixty yards, the strength of an army sustaining attack was more than quadrupled, provided they had force enough to man the entrenchments as well." Grant would throw the *Army of the Potomac* against lines such as these, again and again despite their apparent strength.

At first, Grant substituted using a direct attack, such as had failed at Laurel Hill, with attempting to somehow get around one of his enemy's flanks. This plan was primarily in response to perceived aggressive activity by Lee. Word of Willcox's skirmishing on the Fredericksburg Road arrived at Grant's headquarters around 1000 and further news that the division was being threatened nearly two hours later led the general to assume that Lee was attempting to threaten the *Army of the Potomac's* left. Combining this information with dispatches from Hancock that Rebel forces had disappeared from Todd's Tavern,

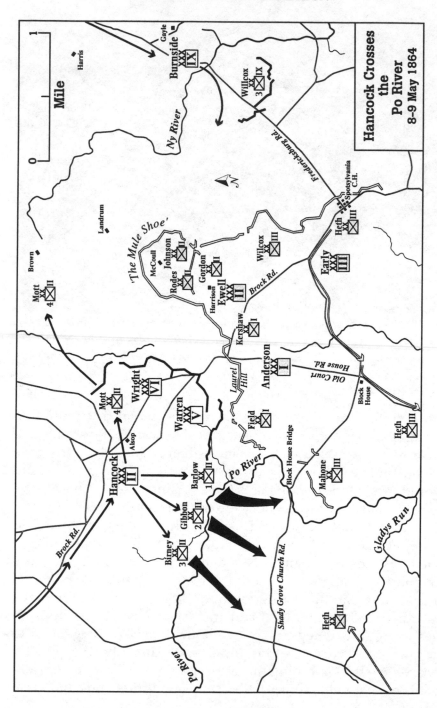

Grant concluded that Lee was, in fact, weakening his left to operate northeast of Spotsylvania to threaten Burnside, a fear confirmed by an erroneous dispatch arriving at 1245 that Willcox was now under heavy attack. This danger to Burnside also contained an opportunity for Grant, for if the enemy was weakening his left to undertake an assault elsewhere, a force might be able to turn that enemy flank and get between Lee's army and Richmond. To counter Burnside's supposed peril and obtain an opportunity to defeat Lee without a frontal attack, Grant ordered Hancock's *II Corps* to probe the Confederate left.

While these moves were taking place on the field around Spotsylvania, Grant received good news from other fronts of the war. Sherman was on the move in northwest Georgia, forcing back Joseph Johnston's *Army of Tennessee* and currently threatening the city of Resaca. Closer to Grant, Butler had landed at City Point, Virginia and was now moving against the Petersburg Railroad, a vital rail link for the Confederate capital of Richmond. In the Shenandoah Valley, Sigel was moving south, apparently ready to claim the region for the Union. According to Porter, if Grant was enthusiastic about his good fortune so far, he did not show it, "General Grant did not express any particular gratification regarding these reports except the one from Sherman, and in fact made few comments about them." Grant also took time on the ninth to send a note to Halleck explaining the slowness of his advance, "My movements are terribly embarrassed by our immense wagon train. It could not be avoided however."

Meanwhile, Hancock was attending to his mission which turned out to be a trek through several natural obstacles that could play havoc with an infantry movement. The primary of these was the Po River, a waterway snaking its way to the southwest, leaving an s-like curve, the middle of which was the location where the Confederate line was anchored. This meant that Federal troops would have to make at least two crossings of the river if they were to get successfully around the enemy's flank. At 1800, Hancock had his troops make their first crossing at three different points along the Po. Pontoon bridges were laid

Where bridges did not exist or could not be repaired, the numerous small rivers of northern Virginia required the use of pontoons, such as these of Hancock's II Corps. *A pontoon train formed part of any major army of the time.*

and the troops pressed on toward Shady Grove Church Road and then east for the Block House Bridge for their second crossing. Dense woods and oncoming darkness hampered the speed of the movement, denying Hancock the opportunity to get across the Po that day. While *II Corps* troops reached the bridge, in the general's opinion it was much too late to make it across to the other bank, "I was anxious to reach the bridge on the Block House road, take possession of it and effect a crossing of the river before halting, but it was found impracticable to

The Union army's Brigadier General Orlando B. Willcox.

keep the skirmish line moving through the dense woods in the darkness though a portion of the skirmishers reached the river, which was ascertained too deep for fording. I was therefore compelled to wait until morning." The general reported his situation to Humphreys at 2200 leaving the responsibility for the continuation of advance with his superiors, "Knowing that General Grant's intention was for the column to move on, I can still give the order, but do not think it wise, and await your instruction." The order to move forward was not given, a mistake perhaps, since the enemy was making adjustments to guard against the threat Hancock posed.

Actually, the hazards to the *IX Corps* that sent Hancock on his mission never existed. The forces Union Brigadier General Willcox had contended with belonged to a division of Confederate Third Corps troops, belonging through a trick of fate to a general with a similar name, Major General Cadmus Wilcox. These were going into position to cover the Fredericksburg

The Confederate army's Major General Cadmus M. Wilcox.

Road, not to threaten Burnside's flank. Thus, the resulting confrontation between the Federal Willcox and the Confederate Wilcox had been blown out of proportion. But while Lee had not dispatched forces from his left to his right, during the evening of the ninth he was now, in fact, doing the opposite, ordering Early to send one of his divisions to the Shady Grove Road to defend the Block House Bridge. Brigadier General William Mahone's division was dispatched to meet the order arriving a few hundred yards east of the Block House Bridge just as the morning of 10 May began to break. Later, Lee had Early send another division to the vicinity of the Block House Bridge and Major General Henry Heth's was dispatched.

The stage was now set for a confrontation on the next day on the banks of the Po.

Butler's Bermuda Hundred Campaign

Every Union advance against Richmond ran up against the same problem, how to move and supply a large army across the terrain of northern Virginia where dense forests and rivers impeded maneuvers while enemy raiders harassed lines of communications. One seductive solution to these difficulties was to move the army by sea to the Virginia coast and advance from there. Such an operation seemingly nullified the difficulties with the overland route. Supply lines couldn't be harassed because the Confederacy hardly had a navy to speak of. Better still, the distance an army would have to march from a landing point on one of the region's navigable rivers to Richmond would be much shorter than any route over land. But even this grand design contained a vital flaw; without a major force in Northern Virginia, Washington, D.C. appeared vulnerable to an enemy attack. Union political and military leaders holding this belief hampered Union Major General George B. McClellan's seaborne advance against Richmond in 1862 and denied Grant the opportunity to make a similar move when he planned his offensives for 1864. However, if Grant could not make such an offensive with the larger part of the forces under his command, maybe a smaller one could threaten the Confederate capital, thus diverting enemy attention and troops from his main force as it operated between Washington and Richmond. The idea became the basis for one of the several advances Grant planned for May 1864 to erode the Southern capacity to wage war.

Charged to undertake this part in the operation was the *Army of the James* under Benjamin Butler. Like Franz Sigel, commander of Grant's offensive in the Shenandoah Valley, Butler was a military novice who rose to high command by benefit of his political clout. Butler's force, based east of Richmond at Yorktown and Gloucester, consisted of 39,000 men of the *X Corps* under Major General Quincy Gillmore and the *XVIII Corps* under Major General William F. "Baldy" Smith. Most of his troops were confident in the success of their mission and eager to participate in this part of the May offensives.

On 2 May, Butler was notified of Grant's intention to get the *Army of the Potomac* under way on 4 May and was told to have his own troops transported up the James River as far as they could go that night. Butler had chosen Bermuda Hundred as the area of his operations, a peninsula of land bounded by the James River to the north and the Appamattox River to the south. Once there, Butler's troops would be 15 miles away from Richmond and less than 10 miles from the strategically vital rail terminus of Petersburg. His army was in motion in the early morning hours of 5 May despite delays and he landed on Bermuda Hundred that afternoon and evening without meeting any opposition.

The absence of any enemy opposition was largely because, at first, there were only a few troops that the Confederates could muster to meet this threat. Commanding them were the various castoffs of several theaters and battles, generals noted for their command ability, but who for various reasons had been purged from more illustrious duties to find themselves commanding troops in the backwaters of the war. Overseeing Confederate forces south of the James River was General Pierre Gustave Toutant Beauregard, commander of the bombardment of Fort Sumter who had later fought at First Bull Run, Shiloh and Corinth. One of his aides was Major General Daniel Harvey Hill who had fought with the Army of Northern Virginia and then the Army of Tennessee before his difficulties with its commander lost him his division and brought him back to Richmond. Beauregard's district commander facing Butler was George Pickett, whose charge at Gettysburg on 3 July 1863 has become so infamous. As Butler was advancing up Bermuda Hundred, these men were scrambling to concentrate a force from scattered commands to meet the threat the Union general posed.

Butler's corps were on the road on 6 May trudging for positions where they would build fortifications across the peninsula before continuing their offensive. Butler then made swipes against the Petersburg and Richmond Railroad, skirmishing with enemy forces and sending his cavalry on raids against the railroad as well. He initially maneuvered against Petersburg on 9 May only to run into the obstacle of a Confederate division under Brigadier General Bushrod Johnson at Swift Creek. Continual fear that the Army of Northern Virginia might fall on him from the north kept Butler from moving more aggressively. Instead of attempting to move around Johnson as his subordinates suggested, the cautious Butler was content with having his troops destroy more of the railroad. News from Stanton arrived on the night of 9 May telling Butler, falsely, that the Army of Northern Virginia was retreating for Richmond under pursuit from Grant. Thinking it might be best to link up with the *Army of the Potomac*, Butler had his army return to their trenches before beginning a march against Richmond on 12 May.

Butler's inability to act with more decisiveness allowed the Confederates to organize a force to fend off his blow whenever it did come. With Beauregard ill, the task of scraping up forces to put in the field fell upon poor Pickett. The major general only had a paltry force of a regiment, an artillery battalion, and some reserves and militia to head off the *Army of the James* when it landed on Bermuda Hundred on 5 May. In two days though, enough forces had been funneled to him to number 3,500 men, still not enough to stop his powerful enemy should he decide to act decisively, but more than ample to instill in Butler a fateful taste for timidity. All Pickett's hard work eventually overpowered him with exhaustion, forcing the general to leave his command. By that time, Beauregard had 20,000 men in two divisions under his command and moved forward on 11 May to meet the enemy bearing down on Richmond.

The scene was set for battle when *Smith's Division* in the advance made contact with Confederate forces the night of 12 May at Drewry's Bluff. Gillmore's corps came up and both maneuvered the enemy out of his advance works toward their stronger defenses in the rear. For the next two days, not much was done by both sides except some sparring for position and digging in. Meanwhile, Beaureguard was interested in more aggressive ideas. He lobbied with Confederate President Jefferson Davis to have Lee join with his forces so they could defeat Butler together and then go against the *Army of the Potomac*, a fantastic scheme which the president wisely rejected. He did, however, give his assent to Beauregard's planned attack on Butler's position at Drewry's Bluff. Beauregard initially wanted to wait until 18 May, but his superiors urged him to move forward earlier. His attack was to take place on the morning of the 15th.

The day began with a thick fog covering the field, confusing soldiers on both sides once the fighting began. The Confederates gained the upper hand when Major General Robert Ransom's force of 6,400 managed to get on the Federal flank and destroy a brigade there, capturing its commanding officer and hundreds of men. The fog continued to confound generals and commanders on both sides. Major General Robert F. Hoke's Confederate division was supposed to link up with Ransom's command, but couldn't locate it and hit the Federal lines alone. Hoke suffered heavy casualties, some of his troops getting stuck in wire entanglements the Yankees had put in front of their entrenchments. Worse still, two brigades under Major General W.H.C Whiting might have given the Confederates the strength to press the attack home never arrived. Even though the tide of battle was turning, Major General Smith was still under the belief that he was getting bloodied and ordered his troops to retreat. When the fog finally cleared a bit, he saw he was in error and countermanded his order. Gillmore for his part was paralyzed by the confused events. Charged to undertake an assault and coming under sporadic attacks himself, the general complained about a lack of support, prepared to attack and then pulled back when the *XVIII Corps* retreated again. The battle ended with Beauregard being left with the Federal entrenchments and a victory of sorts, though not a great one, inflicting 4,160 casualties while suffering around 2,500.

With Drewry's Bluff being a mess, Butler decided to retreat back to his original defenses at Bermuda Hundred. Beauregard followed, arriving there on 17 May. His forces effectively nullified the strength of Butler's command by digging fortifications across the neck of the peninsula, effectively corking the *Army of the James* in a bottle from which it could do no further harm. Another of Grant's offensives had come to naught. Instead of keeping the enemy pinned down, Grant had lost hundreds of troops from his use. Butler held command until November of 1864.

The Gold Hoax of 1864

After Grant began his great Overland Campaign against Richmond, news on his activities was pretty sparse, even to the highest officials in Washington. Lincoln himself admitted that he had little idea what his head general was up to in Virginia, telling one visitor, "...Grant has gone to the Wilderness, crawled in, drawn up the ladder, and pulled in the hole after him, and I guess we'll have to wait until he comes out before we know just what he's up to." However, one reporter had decided that if he could not get news from the front, he would just as well make it up himself. Not only that, he would make himself a pretty sum for the effort.

The Civil War provided a certain correspondent named Joseph Howard with the opportunity to cultivate a flamboyant reputation for himself. As a reporter covering some of the early battles for the *New York Times*, he displayed an uncanny ability to grab a scoop and, failing that, the imagination to create one. Howard had the distinction of concocting the widely circulated, and believed, story that Lincoln had snuck into Washington in a disguise for his 1861 inaugural. He later managed to get an eyewitness account of the closed funeral of the fallen Un-

ion hero Major General Philip Kearny, killed at the battle of Chantilly in 1862, by disguising himself as a Catholic priest. Another of his more disreputable deeds was his occupation of a telegraph wire with dispatches of Biblical passages to deny its use to competing newsmen.

By 1864, Howard was city editor for *The Brooklyn Eagle*, a relatively prestigious position which did not prove to his liking. Bored and resentful from being turned down for positions with other newspapers, the newspaperman decided to play a practical joke on his compatriots. With the help of an *Eagle* reporter, Howard forged an Associated Press dispatch telling of a horrendous disaster which had befallen Grant in the Wilderness, a situation so grim that Lincoln was calling for a day of fasting and the conscription of 400,000 troops. Howard also sought to make some money off the scam. He had invested quite a few dollars in gold which would become even more precious when word of the supposed disaster hit the streets.

The fake dispatches were distributed to several New York papers including the *Herald*, *World*, *Daily News*, *Times*, *Tribune* and *Journal of Commerce*. A cautious editor for one of the papers perceived foul play was afoot and contacted the Associated Press to confirm the story. When AP denied the dispatch, he got the word out of the hoax, but not before the morning edition of *The Journal Commerce* and *The World* hit the streets with the phony story. Horace Greely's famed *Tribune* was more fortunate, it had printed 20,000 copies before being informed of the ruse, all of which were destroyed before any damage could be done to the reputation of that paper.

Howard's story did manage to create a brief stir, causing the stock market to dip and gold to soar 10 percent, but the fact that other papers had not bought into the scam calmed the commercial world. Political leaders were understandably upset, however, and sought to capture and punish those responsible. Orders were sent to the officer with military jurisdiction over New York, Major General John Dix, to take control of *The Journal Commerce* and *The World* along with the Independent Telegraph Company which had sent out the dispatch. The heavy handed measures brought a howl of protest from journalists and anti-Republican elements.

It wasn't long before the real perpetrators were apprehended, Howard and his accomplice. Both men were committed to Fort Lafayette for three months before their release, won by the urging of abolitionist preacher Henry Ward Beecher. Howard's betrayal of his profession did not end his journalistic career; he continued to write after the war, even getting a syndicated column, and became president of the New York Press Club. Noted French science fiction author Jules Verne paid Howard a superlative complement by using his audacious personality as the model for characters in his works *Michael Strogoff* and *The Special Correspondent*.

CHAPTER IV

"They Were Like Sheep Being Led to the Slaughter"

10 May 1864

Grant was aware that his enemy was now on the scene in front of him, well entrenched and waiting for an attack. Such lines that the Confederates were constructing to oppose him should have impressed him with the folly that would result from a frontal attack. However, frustrations throughout the day influenced him to launch unwise assaults up and down the Confederate line on 10 May which had stood no chance of success. For all the senseless fighting and casualties that Grant suffered for his pugnacity that day, he did find a possible opening that might obtain victory if properly played.

The tenth of May began with the Federals of the *II Corps* trying to find a way to safely get across the Po. Hancock found that morning that his original route across the Block House Bridge was obstructed by Confederates of Mahone's Division, south of the Po, who were throwing up works on the high ground overlooking the bridge and strengthening their line with rails. With this crossing blocked, the corps commander set about finding another point to get across the river where the enemy would not hamper his movements. Orders for a reconnaissance worked their way down the chain of command. First, Nelson A. Miles' *First Brigade* of Barlow's division received instructions to search for a crossing. Miles then sent the *61st New York* of his command downstream to investigate and the regiment sent some of its members across the Po where they got into a sharp firefight with the enemy. The New Yorkers quickly retreated across the stream carrying five men wounded during the skirmish. Fortunately for the Federals, a more likely crossing point was discovered. A Lieutenant Robertson of Miles' staff learned about a crossing point at Gladys Run, a tributary of the Po, from a local resident and went out to locate it. On approaching the crossing, Robertson talked with another resident who informed him that the enemy was positioned in strength across the stream, information the lieutenant chose not to believe. He crossed with 20 men anyway only to find the warning had been correct, Rebels were in strength there, men of Heth's Division which had come up on Mahone's left. Other probes revealed the enemy was too numerous and too entrenched to effect a safe and successful flanking maneuver of his left.

The difficulties Hancock faced in his mission now led Grant to consider a change in plan. If Hancock continued his maneuvering it would leave him separated from the rest of the army by a stream that would have to be crossed twice, either by forces coming to reinforce the *II Corps* or *II Corps* troops trying to retreat. Worse still, the forces opposing Hancock pointed to a dangerous concentration of the enemy against him. These realities compelled the attempted flanking maneuver of the Confederate left to be abandoned, but if one opportunity was lost, another one had appeared. Lee had taken troops away from other points in his line to protect his left, Grant assumed, somewhere part of the enemy position must be weak enough to penetrate. An all out attack might yield that information.

Orders were issued for a frontal assault around 1000. Hancock was told to immediately transfer two of his divisions to Warren's position and lead a vigorous combined attack with the *V Corps* to take place punctually at 1700. The remaining *II Corps* division was to be left in a position to threaten the enemy left while at the same time joining the rest of the army in its attack if required. Both the *II Corps* and *V Corps* commanders were given a copy of the same attack order, "General Hancock has been ordered to throw two divisions of his corps on your right, with which and your corps an attack on the enemy will be made at 5 p.m. this day. You will accordingly make all dispositions. Major General Hancock will by virtue of seniority have command of the combined operations." Wright's *VI Corps* and Mott's *II Corps* division on his left were to join the offensive as well, attacking from their positions further north.

From late morning to mid-day, the *II Corps* marched to the tune of its new instructions. Gibbon's and Barlow's divisions were sent to participate in the *V Corps'* attack with the former recrossing the Po to move behind the *V Corps'* right in Crawford's division's rear and with the latter taking position as a reserve. Barlow's division remained across the river to threaten the Confederate left, only to become endangered itself when Heth's force and Mahone's pushed forward across the Gladys Run advanced with his troops, crossing the Po at the Block House Bridge. Originally, Barlow's men were prepared to meet such an attack and had built defenses for that purpose. But Meade became concerned that the division was too vulnerable in such an exposed position and did not want it fighting a battle by itself south of the Po. Orders conflicting with the general attack were dispatched to Hancock, who was by then already with Warren, instructing him to return to the Po and attend to Barlow's withdrawal.

Barlow began to have his forces pull back across the stream around 1400 under the cover of guns from the *II Corps* artillery, protection that was augmented by the arrival of Birney's division an hour later. Their help was needed as Barlow's men increasingly came under enemy artillery bombardment and musketry that began to take a toll. When the Confederate cannon fire erupted, a shell struck Private Enos Shirts of the *105th Pennsylvania*, tearing him to pieces and soaking his nearby comrades in blood. Heth's brigades attacked several times, causing significant casualties, but suffered repulse after repulse.

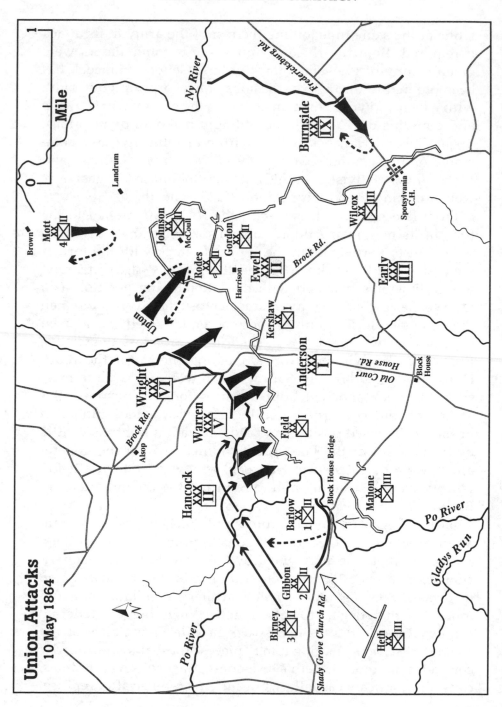

Union Attacks
10 May 1864

V Corps artillery on the Union left flank. Given the deadliness of rifle fire at this stage of the war, the gunners have dug in for protection.

Hancock commended the conduct of Barlow's division during the action, saying that its members retreated, "displaying such coolness and steadiness as are rarely exhibited in the presence of dangers so appalling. It seemed, indeed, that these soldiers were devoted to destruction." Lieutenant Simon Pincus of the *66th New York* agreed, "The men were cool and collected, the firing was rapid and continuous."

Still, despite Barlow's men holding against the attacks, their retrograde movement became increasingly confused and panicky. Some commands never received orders to retreat and calls of "every man for himself" went up when the enemy appeared close to surrounding them. Units quickly broke apart into small groups as men made a swift dash to the rear and safety. The *148th Pennsylvania* never received orders to retire from its brigade commander Colonel John Brooke, supposedly because a messenger could not be sent through the woods which had caught on fire. The colonel of the regiment, James Beaver, suspected something was up when he hadn't received any instructions for an hour and sent a sergeant to his right to investigate. The soldier came back on the run, eyes blazing, and shouted, "Colonel, the rebels are in there." His Pennsylvanians rushed to fall back, fighting to their last cartridge as they went,

II Corps *commander Winfield S. Hancock in the field with his sub-ordinates, the* **First Division's** *Francis C. Barlow, the* **Third Division's** *David B. Birney, and the* **Second Division's** *John Gibbon.*

making it across the river to join the rest of their division. When the fatigued, but safe, Colonel Beaver sank exhausted to the ground on the north bank of the Po, an artillery officer rode up to him and offered a flask of whiskey, "This is what you want, Colonel." Beaver took a sip of what he said was his only drink of whiskey during the war, nearly choking on the alcohol, but becoming instantly revived.

Also during the retreat, a gun of the *1st Rhode Island's Battery A* under Captain William J. Arnold was rammed in between two trees as it was being driven from the field. Axes and other measures were quickly employed to free it and Colonel Brooke was ready to expend every effort to have it carried to safety, but nothing proved successful. Captain Arnold reluctantly said it was no use, the gun would have to be left behind. The fuss over a gun was an important point of honor for up to that point the

II Corps had never lost cannon to the enemy. Captain Arnold's piece would be the first.

Despite such losses, Barlow's division made it safely across the Po, helped by burning woods which kept the enemy at bay. The bridges behind them were pulled up or destroyed and an artillery duel by guns on opposite sides of the river ended the affair. Though of little importance to the campaign itself, the battle on the Po was a matter of some pride to the *II Corps*. After Hancock learned Heth had published a congratulatory order to his troops for their service that day, he recorded bitterly, "Had not Barlow's fine division, then in full strength, received imperative orders to withdraw, Heth's division would have had no cause for congratulations."

With the withdrawal of the *II Corps* from the left of the Confederate army, the *V Corps* now was to attempt a breakthrough against its center, where the Southern troops would enjoy the benefit of strongly entrenched lines. The usually cautious Warren was optimistic of his chances for success and told Meade he could break the enemy's line in his front with his own and some of the *II Corps* troops already up. Meade was willing to have Warren try and around 1530 told Hancock that the possibility of a successful assault by the *V Corps* was so promising, Warren would attack with Gibbon's troops who were already up. *II Corps* troops would still have to be sent to assist, Birney's division was to march to help out in the attack as soon as Barlow's division made it to safety north of the Po.

Warren was going to make his attack with two of his own divisions, Cutler's on the left and Crawford's on the right, with Webb's and Carroll's brigades from Gibbon's *II Corps'* division in the center. However, the *V Corps* commander did not have much reason to be optimistic about the success of his mission. The ground his advance would cross was not ideal for the mass assault envisioned, being cut by a ravine and covered by a thick tangle of trees and underbrush. Gibbon wrote of the path his soldiers would have to take, "The position occupied by these troops was in a dense wood, filled with dead cedar trees, whose hard dry branches, projecting like so many bayonets from the stem, rendered the movement of a line of battle in any sort of order utterly impracticable." Worse still, many of Warren's Yankees were exhausted from skirmishing with the enemy for most of the day. Crawford reported to Warren at 1345 that his men had managed to get so close to the enemy line, that they could not stand up without drawing a volley from the enemy position and concluded with "Our troops suffer in their present position severely." Gibbon's men were also tired from their continuous marching and counter marching throughout the ninth and tenth. Armed with their commander's enthusiasm, faced with strong fortifications and rugged terrain, handicapped by their own exhaustion, the *II* and *V Corps* began their attack some time after 1600.

The troops battled as best they could through the trees, their lines becoming disorganized as they advanced. Cutler's men came up in two lines against Law's Brigade; the Yankee formation was further disorganized by cannon fire and musketry and staggered to a halt. Brigadier General James Rice of Cutler's *Third Brigade* tried to bring up the second line to push forward only to be mortally wounded. While dying at a hospital, he was asked if there was any way he might rest more easily. "Turn me with my face toward the enemy," was his reply. Some of the soldiers in Cutler's first line broke, stampeding through the *24th Michigan* of the elite *Iron Brigade* and cracking that regiment as well. A member of the *150th Pennsylvania* wrote bitterly, "To mount the farther slope through the dense forest and to dislodge an enemy numerous and well posted, with protecting breastworks was no holiday task. The attack failed, as might have been foreseen, and Warren recoiled with heavy loss." Gibbon's troops on Cutler's right fared no better. Webb reported that his men had had time to observe the ground for their attack and had convinced themselves it was hopeless. Crawford's men were fortunate enough to advance over open terrain with artillery support, but were likewise exposed to enemy fire and suffered from it. Attacking John Gregg's Texas Brigade, they too could make no headway against the enemy.

Hancock arrived at 1730 to take control over the demoralizing

Brigadier General Lysander Cutler's **Fourth Division** *of the* **V Corps** *included his old command, the* **6th Wisconsin** *of the* **Iron Brigade.**

affair. An hour later, he received orders to launch another attack and prepared to do so though his dispositions were interrupted by headquarter fear of an enemy force attempting to flank the Federal army's right. Hancock sent troops to investigate, but the threat proved groundless and attention was given once again to breaking through the Confederate line, this time with Cutler's, Gibbon's, and Crawford's divisions moving forward with two brigades each and Brigadier General J.H. Hobart Ward's *First Brigade* of Birney's *II Corps* division on the march as well.

The morale in the assaulting columns was not high. A nearly unanimous feeling of the attack's futility ran through the rank and file of the troops participating in the attack, a belief that they were being led to slaughter. Nothing was done to allay their concerns as Pennsylvanian Charles Banes in Owen's brigade of Gibbon's division recalled, "In spite of the horrible losses required by the obedience to this command, there was an approach to the ridiculous manner of its communication. No officer of higher rank than a brigade commander had examined the approaches to the enemy's works on our front, and the whole expression of the person who brought the message seemed to say, 'The general commanding is doubtful of your success.' The moment the order was given, the messenger put to spurs and rode off, lest by some misunderstanding the assault should begin before he was safe out of range of the enemy's responsive fire." The doomed attack began in the evening hours around 1900.

Cutler's brigades struggled through the wood once more and got up close to Law's troops who were expecting the attack and were waiting to deliver their muskets' loads with deadly effect. Before the Federals marched forward, Southern soldiers had gone out in front of their trenches before the attack to collect ammunition cartridges from the dead and wounded and many now had an extra loaded musket at hand. Some were even taunting the Yankees to make it a little closer to the Confederate works during their next charge so the Rebels would not have so far to go to rake the dead and wounded for clothes, shoes, and muskets. The Federals tried to meet this challenge, fighting on while the dead and wounded were left to be burned when woods caught fire, but they could not break through the enemy's entrenchments. Gibbon's brigades advanced a short distance, quickly coming under heavy fire that took a severe toll. A soldier in the *39th Massachusetts* wrote, "Grape and canister plowed through our ranks. Both colorbearers were shot down, and for a moment our line melted away; but other hands grasped the colors, and we renewed the charge, only to be again repulsed. No army on earth could capture the works with such odds against it, but we charged once more, then gave up." A Pennsylvanian wrote that the attack of his unit was carried out without much spirit, "The men had weighed the probabilities of success and decided that the attempt was hopeless. The advance along the lines was made without enthusiasm, and it continued only a short distance, when a halt was made and firing commenced and continued for a brief period, when the whole force fell back as suddenly as before." Crawford was more successful, though not by much, only gaining ground in front of G.T. Anderson's Georgia Brigade. Most of Hobart Ward's brigade, pitching into John Gregg's Texans and Arkansasians in a massed column, was not as lucky as J.D. Bloodgood of the *141st Pennsylvania* recalled:

> The troops had witnessed the failure of Warren's men to take the ridge and the terrific slaughter which resulted, and moved forward with a good deal of reluctance, for they were like sheep being led to the slaughter. The word of command, however, had gone forth, and they must obey even to death. In solid lines onward they sweep toward that fatal crest, when suddenly from the dusky muzzles of thousands of rebel muskets leap crimson tongues of fire, and the deadly bullets come crashing through our ranks, covering the earth with uniformed bodies. But still those lines move on with unfaltering step till those huge guns, shotted to the very muzzle with grape and canister and trained with deadly precision upon the advancing columns, belch forth their death-dealing contents into the very faces of our boys, mowing great gaps in those already decimated lines. Then our columns halt, waver, advance, halt again, then waver as if in uncertain balance, then break into a wild, disorderly retreat, and rush for a place of safety, continuing their flight till they are safely behind their line of works.

But a modicum of success was won on this part of the line by the Federals. Some of the Southerners there had thought their day of fighting over before the attack, many were so completely exhausted they could not rouse themselves to meet the enemy when he came on again, while others were cooking their meals. Members of the *86th New York* and *3rd Maine* climbed into the unprepared enemy's works to do battle. There was some hand to hand combat that drove away some of the Confederates before a counterattack by John Gregg's and some of G.T. Anderson's men along with canister from nearby guns forced the Federals to retreat. During the fight Confederate Colonel Robert Taylor was forced to rely on a frying pan to defend himself and rally his troops when he found his sword not at hand. It was said that some of his men bore a back ugly band on the cheek from that pan for allowing the enemy to surprise him and ruin the meal he was then cooking.

After this attack was repulsed, another attempt was planned; fortunately it was called off to the relief of the troops who had toiled so fruitlessly against the strong Confederate position all afternoon. Eugene Nash of the *44th New York* wrote of the news, "Eager ears were listening to hear the initiative moment. On such occasions the mind is usually active in endeavoring to anticipate what the outcome will be. Anxious moments passed, but no signal came. The order was finally countermanded and the mental tension that prevailed was relaxed. No regrets were expressed when it became known that the movement had been abandoned, as there was considerable uncertainty about what the result would be." Some 5,000 Union troops might have been lost during the failed attacks while the Confederate lines stood just as formidable as ever. No advantageous result had been won for so expensive a cost in blood.

While the *II* and *V Corps* assaults proved fruitless, Horatio G. Wright's *VI Corps* enjoyed a brief, but significant moment of success. Outside the projecting bulge in the Confederate line occupied by Johnson's division, Wright's replacement as commander of the *First Division*, Brigadier General David Russell had personally inspected the ground and found a weakness. Russell was a veteran of many fields, but his single most important success was the capture of 1,600 Confederate troops by a surprise attack at Rappahannock Station the year before. Spotsylvania gave Russell and a talented subordinate of his the chance to exhibit similar daring. After Confederate skirmishers had been driven out of the woods west of the angle and into their own lines a path was discovered leading through the wood, over 200 yards of ground directly to the enemy line. Russell felt a force of massed infantry might be able to make a surprise charge from the wood to the enemy position and break

Emory Upton

through it. Wright approved the plan and 12 regiments, altogether a force of some 5,000 men, were gathered for its execution. The commander charged to undertake the plan was a 24-year-old colonel, Emory Upton.

Upton and the regimental commanders both surveyed the ground over which their charge would take place. The works that they would assault were formidable, before them lay a network of abatis, followed by the traverses, surmounted by heavy logs underneath which were slits where troops could fire from relative safety. Several well-placed artillery pieces would strengthen the destructive fire power that could come from those defenses. And worse still, about 100 yards behind these works, another line of fortifications was being constructed.

To take these lines, Upton gave his men a complex series of instructions. He organized his force into a formation of four lines of three regiments each in the following manner:

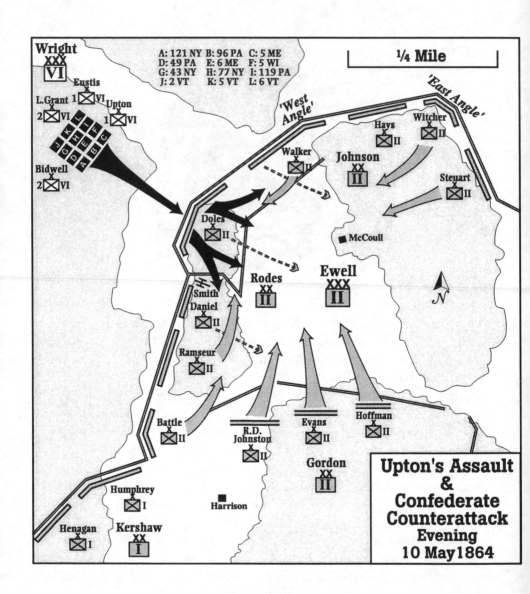

Wright
XXX
VI

A: 121 NY B: 96 PA C: 5 ME
D: 49 PA   E: 6 ME   F: 5 WI
G: 43 NY   H: 77 NY I: 119 PA
J: 2 VT   K: 5 VT   L: 6 VT

¼ Mile

'East Angle'

Eustis
XX VI

L.Grant 1 XX VI   Upton
2 XX VI   1 XX VI

'West Angle'

Witcher
XX II

Hays
XX II

Walker
XX II

Johnson
XX
II

Steuart
XX II

Bidwell
2 XX VI

Doles
XX II

McCoull

N

Rodes
XX
II

Ewell
XXX
II

Smith
Daniel
XX II

Ramseur
XX II

Battle
XX II

Evans
XX II

Hoffman
XX II

R.D.
Johnston
X II

Humphrey
XX I

Gordon
XX
II

Harrison

Henagan
XX I

Kershaw
XX
I

Upton's Assault
&
Confederate
Counterattack
Evening
10 May 1864

5th Me.	96th Pa.	121 N.Y.
5th Wis.	6th Me.	49th Pa.
119 Pa.	77 N.Y.	43d N.Y.
6th Vt.	5th Vt.	2nd Vt.

These were to advance for the enemy works without stopping to fire. The troops were to advance with bayonets fixed. Only the first line would approach with their guns loaded and capped, the rest would advance with their pieces loaded, but not capped to deprive them of the urge to fire instead of charging. When the works were carried the *96th Pennsylvania* and the *121st New York* would turn to the right to capture a battery. The *5th Maine* would turn to the left to enfilade the enemy line there. The second line would take the works and then halt, firing toward their front. The third would lie down behind the second and the fourth would wait in the woods to be used as the situation demanded. Three *VI Corps* batteries were to bombard the enemy lines 10 minutes before the infantry advanced with the halt in their fire being the signal to move forward. The attack was to begin at 1700, but was delayed for an hour. The troops picked for the attack moved quietly into position for their movement and patiently waited for the signal for their charge. When the cannons finally stopped their bombardment, the infantry swept forward.

The Yankees clambered forward with a mighty hurrah covering the open ground before them in a matter of minutes. For the most part, the enemy in the salient was surprised by the rush, but some alert soldiers did get off enough shots to put the oncoming column under a frontal and flanking fire. It was not enough to stop Upton's men. The lead troops of the first line climbed the works before Doles' Georgians where they were shot down with head wounds from the troops within. Others leapt up to take their places, some hurling their bayonetted muskets like spears. Upton wrote of the battle to take the trenches, "The struggle only lasted but a few seconds. Numbers prevailed, and like a resistless wave, the column poured over

95

the works, quickly putting hors de combat those who resisted, and sending to the rear those that surrendered."

However, while success was at hand, the Union assaulting column had lost its organization and the troops could not meet the precision of their planned movements. Some troops went to the left to take on the Stonewall Brigade, sending the 2nd Virginia and 33d Virginia fleeing for the rear. Others veered to the right to assail B.H. Smith's Virginia battery, capturing several guns, and swept up a couple hundred North Carolinians from the flank of Daniel's Brigade in the bargain. Still others moved straight on ahead to take the Confederate supporting works. Reinforcements were desperately needed if the surprise attained was to be maintained. Upton wrote of this desperate moment, "The enemy's lines were completely broken and an opening had been made for the division which was to have supported our left, but it did not arrive."

The colonel was speaking of Mott's *II Corps* division which was supposed to attack from its position on the left rear of the *VI Corps*. The failure of the command to contribute was not so much Mott's fault since conflicting orders from his superiors had placed him in a difficult situation. While he was under Wright's command and was to participate in Upton's attack, he was also directed to maintain the *Army of the Potomac*'s connection with Burnside at the same time, around two and a half miles away, and be ready to assist the *IX Corps* should it come under attack. Mott complained that his connection with Burnside had depleted his strength since hundreds of his men were detached as skirmishers to maintain that link. This left him with a weak attack force of between 1,200 to 1,500 men in all. If he called in his pickets to strengthen his ranks, he could not safely say that he would be able to attack at the appointed hour. To compound difficulties, while Mott had an important role to play in Upton's attack, no one was too confident in his ability to drive his troops to victory. His command had been active most of the day skirmishing with the enemy, which must have taken a toll on his constitution, for staff officers who visited with him described his condition as lazy, confused and stupid. Wright told Mott to

Gershom Mott, **II Corps, Fourth Division;** *another Union commander whose reputation did not survive the Spotsylvania campaign.*

do the best he could by attacking at 1700 with what forces he had and to use his artillery to demoralize the enemy while invigorating the attacking Yankees. The corps commander concluded his dispatch with, "I rely very much on the effect of your attack."

There is not much to say about Mott's attack save that it failed completely. Not getting word of the delay in the *VI Corps* attack, Mott had advanced around 1700, an hour before the main attack had gotten under way. When his troops did advance, they had to cover 500-600 yards of open terrain while under fire from 22 enemy guns. Mott's hapless units quickly melted under a destructive fire of canister. The survivors were routed and broke for the rear. Mott's swift defeat meant that Upton's troops were on their own.

Another potential source of assistance for Upton was Burnside's *IX Corps.* Grant, at 1030, had attempted to impress Burnside with the need to participate in the general attack taking place at 1700, writing, "...if you have any possible chance of attacking their [the enemy's] right do it with vigor and all the force you can bear. Do not neglect to make all the show of force

Perhaps haunted by past losses, General Ambrose Burnside failed to perform aggressively at Spotsylvania, his last chance to rebuild his military reputation.

you can as the best co-operative effort." For much of the day, the befuddled Burnside dithered over how many divisions he should actually employ in an attack, switching between concentrating all three divisions in an assault from the Gayle house or sending a division to back up Mott while the other two made a demonstration against the enemy right. Grant told Burnside that he probably would not get all his divisions up in time to make the attack and should do the best he could with what was available, "I will leave it to your judgement whether it will be best to attack with your two divisions as they are, or whether one of them should be sent to Mott. As the attack is to be general, however, I incline to the opinion you will be secure in attacking as you are."

When Burnside finally got around to advancing, it was 1800 and even then the general was only interested in a reconnaissance in force rather than a major attack. His troops advanced down the Fredericksburg Road and then merely entrenched. Had Burnside been a bit more aggressive, he might have found out he had gained a major advantage; his forces had in fact turned the Confederate right and were only a few hundred yards from Spotsylvania Court House. However, the corps was now also separated from the rest of the army and vulnerable to attack as well. Orders were given for Burnside to fall back a mile forcing him to give up the precious ground taken. While Grant blamed himself for this incident, writing, "I attach no blame to Burnside for this, but I do to myself for not having had a staff officer with him to report to me his position" he attached his failures of the day to the inability of Mott and Burnside to get "heartily" engaged.

While Upton failed to receive any assistance, the Confederate command directed forces with methodical precision to seal and patch up the breach the enemy had made. Brigadier General James Walker, on the right of the breakthrough, rallied his men and got them firing against the Yankees while Witcher leading Jones' Brigade came up on their left. Steuart also came up to Upton's left preventing Upton's men from advancing further while being unsuccessful in their efforts to push them back. Corps commander Ewell also came on the scene and ordered some of Daniel's North Carolinians to retake Smith's captured guns. Men from Gordon's Division along with Battle's Brigade marched up out of the Army of Northern Virginia's reserve to join in the effort, sweeping the Yankees away. Once the guns were retaken, cannoneers sent by Lee to replace those that were captured earlier in the fight worked the pieces against the enemy. The swiftness of the Confederate response bespoke an incredible professionalism of the veteran Army of Northern Virginia which was seldom matched on any field of the Civil War.

Upton himself did not have any troops to call upon for help against such a swift and efficient reaction. The last of his own

Nearly 1200 Confederate prisoners are run back to Union lines at the double after Upton's attack in an eyewitness sketch.

reserves had advanced into the works and were now fighting against the enemy's counterattacks. With darkness gathering, all Upton could do was hold on until he could retreat his forces in the night or hope reinforcements arrived to help. General Russell opted for the latter course and gave instructions for the attack force to withdraw. Upton's temporary success had cost 1,000 men with some regiments suffering particularly severely. The *5th Maine* lost all of its captains except one and nearly half the *49th Pennsylvania* was gone, including its colonel and lieutenant colonel. Upton gave this summary of his men's efforts during the attack, "They went forward in perfect confidence, fought with unflinching courage, and retired only upon the receipt of a written order, after having expended the ammunition of their dead and wounded comrades." Perhaps only 100 of the enemy were killed, though an extraordinary amount were captured, around 1,000-1,200 Confederates being brought into Union lines.

All around, 10 May had been a day of lost opportunities and fruitless bloody attacks for the Union army. Grant however was giving no thought to retreat. Earlier in the day he had boldly told Halleck his only intention was to advance, claiming, "I shall take no backward steps" and "We can maintain ourselves at

An original sketch of Confederate prisoners during Upton's attack turned into a lithograph for Northern newspapers. In the final version, the Confederates are more skulking.

least and beat Lee's army I believe" as well as requesting more ammunition and 10,000 men from the defenses of Washington D.C. The bad experiences of his failed attacks against the impressive Confederate defenses had not swayed him from advancing south from Spotsylvania either. Upton's temporary success against the salient inspired him to use similar tactics to those employed during that assault, only the next time it would be on a far grander scale.

Emory Upton

Emory Upton, one of the more brilliant military minds to emerge from the Civil War, was born near Batavia, New York in 1839. A serious young man who never drank, smoked and rarely laughed, he began his college schooling at an unlikely place, Oberlin College, Ohio. However, Upton approached his studies with the intention of transferring to West Point and two years later he entered the Military Academy, eventually graduating eighth in the class that graduated the year the Civil War broke out. Afterwards, he was commissioned in the *5th U.S. Artillery*.

Upton served in the first major campaign of the war that led to Bull Run and there aimed and fired the gun which opened the battle. He continued to fight with the artillery through the Peninsula Campaign and the Antietam Campaign. After the battle of Antietam, Upton was slated to return to West Point to teach cadets, an option which was not all pleasing to his aggressive nature. Instead, Upton switched services by joining the volunteers and took command of infantry troops as the colonel of the *121st New York*. Upton won the respect of his troops, but led them on a destructive charge at Chancellorsville which cost him half his command as casualties. The young officer was still eager for combat, so much so that when he took brigade command in time for the battle of Gettysburg he marched his troops as quickly as possible to the action, only to just miss a chance to participate. At Rappahannock Station in November of 1863, Upton displayed his military prowess when he cleverly led an attack which captured a number of rebels, their fortifications and a pontoon bridge.

However, it was at Spotsylvania that Upton achieved his greatest success, winning distinction and praise for his attack and temporary breakthrough of the Confederate line on 10 May 1864. His use of a tight attacking infantry column rushing the enemy line in a sledgehammer assault set the stage for the next Union attack on 12 May. Upton's temporary success won him a field promotion from Grant to the rank of brigadier general. His participation in a charge at Cold Harbor on 1 June 1864 was not as successful; there he lost 230 men in less than a minute.

Upton later served with Phil Sheridan in his 1864 campaign down the Shenandoah Valley, attaining divisional command until a wound knocked him out of his leadership role. The young officer returned to fighting as soon as he could, this time taking command as a major general of cavalry troops under Major General James Wilson in the Western Theater. He fought in Alabama and Georgia before the close of the war.

Upton's post war activities included adopting lessons from the Civil War and European techniques to modernize the American military. He was also critical of the citizen soldier and civilian influence in the U.S. armed forces and argued the need for a strong regular army under professional control. Tragically, Upton suffered from painful headaches as well as bitterness and disillusionment. In 1881, he took his own life with a Colt .45 pistol. His greatest legacy was authorship of two influential classic textbooks of American military thought, *Infantry Tactics* and *Military Policy of the United States*.

Ambrose Burnside

Probably more famous for his magnificent sideburns than his leadership, Ambrose Burnside (1824-1881) grew up in Indiana, the scion of slave owning parents who freed their chattels and moved to the Hoosier State. Young Burnside labored in a tailor shop before his father secured a position at West Point for him which set him on his military career.

Burnside graduated with the class of 1847 and went on to serve in the Mexican War and on frontier posts where he was wounded in action against Apaches. He then left the army in 1853 to undertake a business career in Rhode Island. The enterprising Burnside developed a breech loading carbine which he attempted to sell to the United States government, but met with no success and his venture went bankrupt. (Maybe his ill luck was just a matter of timing since 55,000 of Burnside's guns would be purchased for use in the Civil War.) Fortunately, Burnside's friend and future commander, the dashing George B. McClellan, secured the humbled businessman a job with the Illinois Central Railroad.

Burnside quickly entered the military after the country went to war in 1861. Already a major general in the Rhode Island militia, Burnside organized a regiment and took it to Washington and later commanded a brigade during the Union disaster at First Bull Run on 21 July 1861. A brigadier general after service in that fight, Burnside subsequently took a brigade in a successful expedition on the North Carolina coast, capturing several important ports. His wins there earned him praise from his government, the admiration of the public and a promotion to major general.

In July, 1862, Burnside was recalled to serve with the *Army of the Potomac* under his old friend McClellan. Burnside's performance as commander of the *IX Corps* of the army was lackluster at Antietam, where his force was stalled for several hours trying to cross a creek. Despite this ignominy, the President was a firm believer in Burnside's talents and had the general replace McClellan as commander of the *Army of the Potomac* that November. But Burnside himself did not have complete faith in his own abilities and led the army to a bloody disaster at Fredericksburg, Virginia, on 13 December 1862. The next month he attempted to begin an offensive to flank his enemy's position at Fredericksburg only to have his own army get bogged down in a morass of mud caused by brutal rain and winds. The fiasco became known as Burnside's Mud March and led to his removal from command of the *Army of the Potomac*.

The disgraced general did not go on the shelf, however, but was given command of the *Department of the Ohio* in March 1863, where the general did much to redeem his reputation. During his controversial tenure in that position, he arrested and prosecuted Northern peace activists including the prominent Copperhead Clement L. Vallandigham. He also managed the capture of flamboyant Confederate cavalry raider John Hunt Morgan during his raid through Indiana and Ohio in July of 1863 and thwarted James Longstreet's attempts to take Knoxville, Tennessee.

Burnside returned East once again with these laurels to command the *IX Corps* during Grant's offensive of 1864. His leadership during the battles of the Wilderness and Spotsylvania was adequate at best. After he bungled the attack on the Petersburg Crater on 30 July 1864, the general was removed from command and saw no further service. With the war ending, he resigned his commision on 15 April 1865.

Burnside returned to Rhode Island where he enjoyed more success in business and politics than in war. He served as its governor for three terms and was a Senator for the state in the U.S. Congress.

CHAPTER V

"We Shall Fight It Out On This Line If It Takes All Summer"

10-12 May

On the night of the tenth, strains of music could be heard floating through the woods and over the fields where armies had struggled throughout the day. The tunes were initially mournful, a Confederate band played "Nearer, My God to Thee" leading a Union one to strike up the Dead March from "Saul" Deciding to change the tone of the serenade, the Southern musicians gave a rendition of the rousing "The Bonnie Blue Flag" after which their enemy counterparts responded with "The Star Spangled Banner." Finally both bands played "Home, Sweet Home" winning cheers from listeners on both sides. The happy musical contest belied the life and death struggle that had taken place during the day and briefly turned the soldiers away from the ones yet to come.

Commanders and soldiers were still involved with the important post-battle matters at hand. General Grant took the time to deal out rewards to officers who had performed superbly on the field of battle thus far. He had been given permission to promote officers on the field and now executed this authority by making Upton a brigadier general for his "spirit and dash" during the day's action. In contrast, a general with a critical onus upon him, Gershom Mott, attempted to stir up the patriotic fervor of his troops after their poor performance of the day with a proclamation,

> The brigadier-general commanding is grieved to notice that the Fourth Division, Second Corps, is sacrificing the reputation of "Hooker's old division" (subsequently so ably commanded by Sickles and Berry). There is no excuse for such conduct. The combined armies of the Union are moving at once. Victories are being gained at every point, and the death blow is being dealt to rebellion. The time calls for greater exertion than any previous one, and the commanding general expected it will be put forth. Commanding officers of brigades, regiments, and companies are called upon and enjoined to exercise that example and authority required by them by existing orders and regulations. Let us show it the army and the world that our part has been fully and faithfully performed.

On the other side of the field in the Mule Shoe, Confederate soldiers strove to strengthen their already formidable defenses to avoid a repeat of Upton's attack.

The next morning, Grant wrote to Halleck expressing his satisfaction in the conduct of the campaign and the results attained thus far. No doubt when totalling the casualties from the Wilderness and the fights around Spotsylvania, losses appeared heavy, some 20,000 men and 11 general officers in all. Reinforcements, the general noted, would strongly encourage the depleted ranks of the forces involved in the offensive. At the same time, the lieutenant general maintained his unyielding determination to continue the fight, issuing his famed declaration that he would "fight it out on this line if it takes all summer." This line received the enthusiastic attention of the Northern press which could now report on a general in the East who demanded continual action. One of the reasons Grant could be so bold was his faith that the enemy must be demoralized and ready to crack, "I am satisfied the enemy are very shaky, and are

Ulysses S. Grant and his staff gather on pews taken from the Massaponax Church, shortly after Spotsylvania. Grant sits with his back to the two trees. Horace Porter sits at Grant's right, John Rawlins on his left, flanked by Ely S. Parker. George G. Meade is on the left end of the leftmost pew.

kept up to the mark by the greatest exertions on the part of the officers, and by keeping them in trenches in every position they take." His unrealistic optimism seemed to ignore the battlefield experiences his troops had suffered for the past several days. Their repulses with such heavy casualties by a numerically inferior army did not tell of an enemy that was on the verge of breaking apart. However, Grant could also draw confidence from the victorious word that arrived from campaigns being fought elsewhere. Butler's cavalry had cut the railroads between Richmond and Petersburg, leaving Beauregard separated from the Confederate capital, while Butler himself had won a victory over the Confederate forces opposing him and was safely entrenched in Bermuda Hundred between the James and Appomattox Rivers. Meanwhile, Sheridan was causing havoc in Lee's rear by ripping up track and destroying supplies.

Returning to the situation before him, Grant had been intrigued by Upton's attack and was interested in pursuing the same tactics, but on a much larger scale. He spent the next day reconnoitering the enemy position in order to find the most suitable place for a similar attack to be delivered while Meade solicited his corps commanders for information. At 0730, Meade issued a circular to Hancock, Wright and Warren inquiring about the numbers of men required to hold their present position and the amount that were available for an offensive. Commanders were also to see if troops could be freed for offensive duty through the construction of more defensive works. Any changes in the enemy's lines were to be reported immediately. Meade followed up this circular with a personal conference with each commander. Troops in the field were also to be kept alert and ready. Skirmishers were told to keep close to the enemy lines in order to observe any changes in position or troop movements. In preparation for the offensive, two days rations were issued and soldiers were given ammunition to refill their cartridge boxes. Wagons were dispatched to Belle Plain to bring in more supplies.

Grant became convinced that the Mule Shoe salient was the most advantageous point for an attack and the proper orders for that purpose were issued at 1500. His plan was an intricate series of movements, a reorganization of most of the *Army of the Potomac*, all leading up to a sledgehammer-like blow on the tip of the salient. The *II Corps* would have to do most of the marching and most of the fighting. Hancock was to dispatch Birney's and Barlow's divisions on a trek all the way around Warren's *V Corps* and Wright's *VI Corps* under cover of darkness, eventually taking position on the left of the *VI Corps* and directly a half mile north of the apex of the salient on the fields of the Brown house. Their marching column was to be as compact as possible so there would be no excuse for straggling.

Hancock's remaining division, Gibbon's was too close to the enemy to be removed without notice and would have to remain in its current position until just before daylight at which time it would pull back and rejoin the rest of the *II Corps* if necessary. At 0400 on the twelfth, Birney's and Barlow's men along with Mott would attack in conjunction with Burnside's *IX Corps*. Remembering Burnside's failure to actively participate in the fighting on 10 May, Colonels Orville Babcock and Cyrus Comstock of Grant's staff would assist him on 12 May and impress upon him the importance of advancing. Other staff officers were to keep in communication with *IX Corps* and other portions of Hancock's line. Once a significant lodgement was made, troops were directed to intrench to hold it. Even though clouds began to darken the sky, portending rain, there was to be no postponement of the operation on account of weather.

Wright and Warren were directed to keep their forces as close to the enemy as possible in order to take advantage of any opportunities the attack might present. Warren was also ordered to have his men spread out and take over the trenches vacated by Hancock's men, but was promised support from the *VI Corps* and Colonel J. Howard Kitching's *Heavy Artillery Brigade* to swell his ranks. The only division of the *VI Corps* to man trenches was the one belonging to Ricketts. Russell's and Neill's were to be in the rear ready to move wherever they were needed most.

While orders for the attack were issued in the Federal army, the Army of Northern Virginia adjusted its lines battered by the fighting of the day before and strengthened its position to meet any future enemy offensives. Doles' regiments, ruined by the 10 May attack, were pulled out of line, and ultimately replaced at 1000 by Hay's old brigade of Lousianians under Colonel William Monaghan. Heth returned from the left to the right on the morning of the eleventh since the Federal threat over the Po seemed to have dissipated. The division once again took position in front of the Spotsylvania Court House extending the Confederate line south.

Lee visited that salient early on the eleventh and received

Union dead from early in the Spotsylvania campaign are brought to Fredericksburg for burial.

assurances from his chief engineer Martin Smith that it could be held. Even so, the enemy didn't appear to be making any aggressive moves as division commander Edward Johnson had sent out probes during the day to look for the enemy, but could find nothing. Just in case the enemy intended to attack the Mule Shoe again, Lee gave his subordinates permission to advance toward any attack without waiting for orders and ordered a new line built across the base of the salient.

In the early evening, the Union army implemented the required moves for the next day's offensive. At 1900, *II Corps* division commanders met with Hancock to discuss their part in the grand operation. While they were told they were going to make an attack of the highest importance on the right flank of the enemy, there was nothing the corps commander could tell them about their objective, the numbers of the enemy facing them, the exact plan of attack or why it was going to be made. Regardless, in the late evening hours, most of the corps was on the march.

Barlow, followed by Birney, moved out after 2200, leaving lit fires behind to prevent the enemy from discovering the Federal divisions' disappearance from their front. Orders were given for the men to be extremely quiet with cooking utensils, and canteens were to be arranged to make the least amount of noise and no one was to speak above a whisper. As if to make the movement all the more difficult, the gathering clouds let loose a hard, driving rain. Undaunted, Hancock's men slowly groped their way through the inky darkness of the wet night, stumbling through a wood in mud that was nearly ankle deep. Porter wrote of that miserable night "The condition of the country was such that a horseman could make but slow progress in moving from one point of the field to another. The rain was falling in torrents, the ground was marshy, the roads were narrow, and the movements of the infantry and artillery had churned up the mud until the country was impassable. In the pitch darkness one's horse constantly ran against trees, was shoved off the road by guns or wagons, and had to squeeze through the lines of infantry, who swore like 'our army in Flanders' when a staff officer's horse manifested itself to crawl over them." *II Corps* soldiers vividly recalled that miserable night, a Yank in the *108th New York* writing later, "Nobody knew where we were going, but a rumor was started that we were going back to the rear to rest and wash our clothes. And this was proved partially true, as it rained so hard all night that our clothes were thoroughly washed, but they needed wringing so badly and I think I can safely say that of all our many night marches, this one took the cake. A cold cheerless rain, falling in torrents, mud al la Virginia and just as dark as Egypt. Every man followed his file leader not by sight or touch, but by hearing him growl and swear as he slipped, splashed and tried to pull his pontoons [shoes] out of the mud." The troops were nervous enough knowing as little as they did about their mission, a feeling only intensified by various unsettling incidents. At one point a pack mule laden with cookingware panicked and galloped through the night, a sight John Smith of the *19th Maine* witnessed, "The kettles and frying pans struck the trees along the mule's flight and every few leaps the mule let off panic-stricken brays that could be heard a mile, followed by disemboweled groans, that struck terror to the hearts of the tired soldiers. It seemed for a minute as though a legion of devils armed with frying pans and mounted on mules were charging the Union lines. Some regiments started to run through the woods as though his Satanic Majesty was after them. Fortunately no shots were fired in the excitement and the stampede was soon checked." In another incident, a soldier who accidently discharged his rifle set off nervous fears the column had wandered into enemy lines, a concern that was soon allayed.

Despite the hard night, *II Corps* was moving on schedule. Barlow's division arrived in the vicinity of the Brown House after midnight, allowing his troops to find rest from their exertions. Unfortunately for the division commander, Barlow still had no exact details about the ground he was supposed to cross and the enemy he was supposed to attack. Lieutenant Colonel Waldo Merriam of the *16th Massachusetts* of Mott's command was able to give some general information since he had been involved in the fighting on the tenth and had participated in a reconnaissance on the eleventh, allowing him enough knowledge to sketch out a map of the country *II Corps* was going to have to cross to get to the enemy. Still, the attack's proper path was constructed largely through guesswork. Its direction was determined by a compass on a map from the Brown House to the McCoull house, a structure known to lie within the salient. The hope was that if the Federals marched south from their current position, through a clearing of ascending ground some 400 yards wide and continued on through the fields of the Landrum House, north of the salient, the attackers should eventually hit the enemy line.

It wasn't long before the rest of the *II Corps* joined Barlow and the attacking forces began to set up for their charge. Birney arrived around 0200, and Gibbon, who began his march at 0100, arrived an hour after Birney. Barlow on the left put his men together in a tight column of two lines of two brigades each with the *2nd Delaware* on the left flank of attacking force's front. The first line was held by Brook and Miles and the rear by Smyth and Brown, each 300 men wide and 20 men thick. Birney set his division of two brigades up in a more traditional line formation with Ward on the left and Crocker on the right. Mott had his two brigades behind Birney and Gibbon's division was held in reserve. The ranks were allowed what sleep they could find on the cold wet ground before the time of attack came. Altogether some 19,000 men were assembled on the Brown farm to break through the enemy line.

To the east, Burnside was also preparing his part in the attack of 12 May. His initial moves were rather embarrassing. Having misunderstood his orders, he retreated his men north of the Ny River, destroying the bridge his men used to get across it. Lieutenant Colonel Comstock arrived to point out the error and helped direct the *IX Corps* back to a position where Grant had wanted it to attack from. By 2200, its movements were completed.

As the sledgehammer of *II Corps* manpower awaited the appointed hour for it to sweep down on the Mule Shoe, General Lee himself committed an error of judgement that would seriously weaken his line at the very point the Federals planned to attack. He was misled by intelligence reports indicating a lack of enemy activity or a possible Federal retreat, including word from his second son "Rooney" Lee telling of Federal wagons heading toward Fredericksburg and Burnside's withdrawal to a position above the Ny. In the evening, General Lee told Heth and later Ewell that the Yankees were going to retreat to

Fredericksburg and he wanted the chance to strike a blow when they moved. Heth was directed to ready his troops to march while Ewell was given more specific instructions. Believing the enemy was not present near the Second Corps, Lee felt that Ewell's troops could be easily withdrawn. Ewell asked that the men should be allowed to rest out the rainy night in their trenches, a request Lee granted though he ordered the corps artillery be withdrawn. If the *Army of the Potomac* was retreating, it was important to have those guns out of the salient and over the narrow road in the thick woods behind the salient's lines to ensure they could join a pursuit. Most of the artillery pieces located near the point of the Mule Shoe, up to 10, were limbered up and taken away though four batteries remained in the salient. Soldiers nearby thought the cannons departure could not be a positive development as Confederate McHenry Howard noted, "A little before sunset, we were surprised to notice all the artillery in the salient and on our center, limber up and move to the rear; and asking an officer what this meant, he replied that he did not know, except that they were ordered back to camp. At our headquarters we discussed this movement with great uneasiness, but supposed other batteries would come up to relieve them."

Confederate soldiers passed the evening of the eleventh in the dreary misery caused by the night's cold pounding rain storm. M.S. Stringfellow of the 13th Virginia recalled, "We were made more uncomfortable by the fact that orders came around for 'no fires.' So, rolling up in our oil cloths, we were soon dreaming, perhaps, that the cruel war was over." More disturbing though were the increasing indications that the Federals were not planning to retreat from the area. Shortly after dark, responding to picket reports of an enemy movement, McHenry Howard and another captain in Steuart's Brigade went to the breastworks to investigate. There they heard a distant rumble which they likened to falling water or running machinery. When Steuart was told of this, he notified division commander Allegheny Johnson, "The enemy is moving and probably massing in our front and we expect to be attacked at daylight. The artillery

114

along our front has been withdrawn, by whose orders I do not know and I beg that it be sent back immediately." Johnson reported this news to Ewell who responded that the guns would be returned by 0200. The return of the artillery went too slowly to bode well. It took an hour and half after the guns were supposed to be in position to finally find Second Corps artillery chief Brigadier General Armistead Long and even then, the sleepy cannoneers had to be wakened, horses hitched, and the batteries sent on their way. For his part, Johnson was doing his best to prepare for an attack should one arise. Brigade commanders were alerted to the possibility and he also reported his fears to Gordon who offered him Pegram's Brigade under Colonel John Hoffman. This Johnson chose to position in the reserve works behind the Stonewall Brigade.

In the tip of the Mule Shoe, Johnson's Division was so positioned that it would bear the brunt of the coming *II Corps* attack. On the left, Daniel's Brigade of Rodes' Division was followed by Monaghan's Louisianans, Walker's Virginians of the Stonewall Brigade, York's Louisianans, Witcher's Brigade, and Steuart's Brigade on the far left. Two brigades from Gordon's division, Hoffman's and Evans' commanding Gordon's old brigade, manned reserve works behind the main line. Many of these commands were about to suffer one of the grimmest moments the Army of Northern Virginia had suffered up to that point in the war.

Winfield Scott Hancock

Winfield Scott Hancock's (1824-1886) ability as a corps commander rightfully won him the sobriquet, "Hancock the Superb." His efforts and talents as a leader also made his command, the *II Corps*, one of the elite fighting forces of the Civil War and the shock troops of the *Army of the Potomac*.

Hancock graduated with the West Point class of 1844, ranking 18th among his comrades. He served in a variety of posts in his service before the Civil War, seeing action in the Mexican War and the Seminole War. In 1861, Hancock was serving as post quartermaster in Los Angeles with many soldiers whose sympathies would compel them to side with the Confederacy including Albert Sidney Johnston, Richard Garnett and Lewis A. Armistead. Hancock was eager to get a command in the Union forces, but did not allow his feelings to dissolve his friendship with comrades he would later face on the field of battle. Together they took part in an emotional gathering for farewells before departing to serve on the sides of their choosing in the coming bloodshed. Armistead and Garnett would later lead brigades in Pickett's Charge against men of the *II Corps* under Hancock.

Hancock initially led a brigade of troops with the rank of brigadier general during McClellan's ill-fated Peninsula Campaign and played a leading role in defeating the Confederates at the battle of Williamsburg on 5 May 1862. Later that fall at An-

tietam, Hancock was in division command and later won promotion to major general. He saw action both at Fredericksburg and Chancellorsville, but at Gettysburg, he rendered fine service commanding the left wing of the *Army of the Potomac* during the battle and, on 3 July, oversaw the repulse of Pickett's Charge. During the battle he suffered a slight injury that forced him to leave the field.

After recovering from his injury, Hancock led the *II Corps* through the bloody battles of Grant's Overland Campaign, commanding his troops in major attacks in the Wilderness (4-5 May 1864) and Spotsylvania (12 May 1864). In both, the *II Corps* pierced the enemy line, became disorganized and was forced back by enemy counterattacks. Hancock's Gettysburg wound continued to plague him to the point of driving him from the command of his beloved *II Corps* in November of 1864. He took to various posts during the remainder of the war including command of the *Veteran Reserve Corps*. Immediately after the war, he participated in a campaign to pacify Plains Indians and took command of the 5th Military District during Reconstruction, which gave him command over Louisiana and Texas. Here he exerted a more lenient Reconstruction policy than his predecessor, Philip Henry Sheridan.

Like many of his compatriots, Hancock tried to use his postwar reputation as currency to cash in on a political career and even aspired to the presidency of the United States. Hancock ran as a Democrat in the 1880 election, forcing him into opposition against fellow officers such as Ulysses S. Grant, who sided with fellow Republican James A. Garfield. Garfield defeated Hancock in a narrow contest losing by only 7,000 popular votes. Hancock died on 9 February 1886 and was buried in Norristown, Pennsylvania.

Yellow Tavern and the Death of J.E.B. Stuart

On 8 May 1864, Ulysses S. Grant let loose the hard riding and tough fighting cavalry commander Philip H. Sheridan to raid in the Army of Northern Virginia's rear and threaten the Confederate capital at Richmond. Sheridan's ride might have caused some consternation amongst those who remembered Stoneman's Raid which had taken place almost a year earlier. Back then, Major General Joseph Hooker had unleashed the *Army of the Potomac*'s cavalry under Major General George Stoneman to wreak havoc in the rear of the enemy Army of Northern Virginia. That raid did little to cause the Confederate commander Robert E. Lee any concern. In fact, he simply ignored the move by keeping his own cavalry close by his own army during the battle of Chancellorsville (1-3 May 1863). Lee never had reason to be worried that he made a mistake, Stoneman's troops wrecked some railroad track, but did little else, allowing the whole operation to ranked as a failure. Sheridan was not a Stoneman however, he was a destroying machine. Lee could not afford to have a fighter like that running loose behind his lines.

Sheridan left the *Army of the Potomac* on 9 May with 12,000 cavalry troops and 32 guns heading deep into enemy territory. He did not wait long to cause the Confederates trouble, By nightfall a column of his troops had reached one of Lee's supply bases at Beaver Dam Station where they put loads of Confederate supplies, 100 railway cars, and two locomotives to the torch. Four hundred dejected Union prisoners were also found there and freed. Sheridan continued moving south on 10 May toward Richmond, eventually camping on the banks of the South Anna River.

One of Sheridan's ulterior motives in his advance was to beat the old nemesis of the Union cavalry, the flamboyant Confederate cavalier, James Ewell Brown Stuart. Stuart and his troopers had seemed almost unbeatable early on in the war, almost riding at will into the Union rear lines, destroying supply depots, capturing arms and ammunition, and defeating the Federal troopers that were sent to stop them. By Gettysburg, the situation had changed, the Union cavalry had improved and were even proving a match for Stuart. It was perhaps with the hope of regaining his former glory that the Confederate cavalry commander rode to head off Sheridan and bring him to battle.

Stuart left Lee's army on 9 May with 4,500 men, leaving 3,500 more behind with the Army of Northern Virginia. Stuart drove his column hard to catch up with the enemy, hoping he might be able to join with other forces near Richmond and overwhelm the enemy force through a complex series of attacks. Time and the exhaustion of his troops and their mounts conspired otherwise. Resting his command on the night of 10 May, Stuart had them moving again in the early morning hours of 11 May trying to get between Sheridan and Richmond. The Confederate commander got in front of the Union forces when he reached Yellow Tavern, seven miles north of Richmond, on the Brock Turnpike at 0800. There he drew up his forces into a line to block Sheridan's advance toward the Confederate capital.

Around 1100, a Union brigade arrived and charged the Confederate position only to be thrown back. The pugnacious Sheridan smelled a battle and leapt to the challenge, throwing two divisions against Stuart with one under Brigadier General Wesley Merritt taking the Confederate position head on, while another under Brigadier General James Wilson attempted to get around the enemy right flank. The

Federals charged with Brigadier General George Custer at their head. While taking heavy casualties, the Confederate position began to fracture. Stuart organized a counter attack of 86 men which set the Federals back into retreat. For a while, the battlefield situation was confused and soldiers of both sides intermingled. While Stuart was in the melee, a Michigan soldier spotted him, and seeing his opportunity unloaded a fateful round into Stuart's chest. With Stuart mortally wounded, command devolved upon Robert E. Lee's nephew, Fitzhugh Lee. Both sides continued to fight, but for no result except that Sheridan pulled away to continue for Richmond.

By the time the Federal cavalry reached the Confederate capital, its defenses had been manned, making it a nut that was too tough to crack, so they rode east of the town. Sheridan then attempted to make for the lines of Major General Benjamin Butler's *Army of the James* where he could rest and refit his weary command. Bad weather very nearly made him and his men captives to pursuing Confederate infantry and cavalry forces as mud slowed horses and swollen rivers made for impassable obstructions. Managing to repair the Meadow's Bridge across the Chickahominy River while holding off enemy attacks, Sheridan's command finally reached the safety of Butler's lines on 14 May. All in all he had suffered 625 casualties in giving Confederate military and political leaders a good scare.

But Sheridan's raid had accomplished a very significant goal, the death of J.E.B. Stuart. On the night of 12 May, Stuart's wound was diagnosed as mortal and he was told that he was about to die. The cavalryman resigned himself to God's will, but hoped he might see his wife and child one more time. When two clergymen arrived at 1900, Stuart asked them to join him in singing "Rock of Ages." A half an hour later he passed on, denied his dying wish to see his family who did not arrive until midnight. The repercussions of Stuart's death would be felt in the high command of the Army of Northern Virginia. Upon learning of Stuart's fall, Lee said of his best cavalry commander, "He never brought me a false piece of information."

CHAPTER VI

"The Bayonet Was Freely Used"

12 May 1864

*A*n ominous calm pervaded the early morning gloom near Spotsylvania on 12 May. As if to add a special grimness to the proceedings that were to take place that day, a dense fog hugged the ground, its thickness obscuring the path over which the *II Corps* assaulting columns would march, thus causing Hancock at 0345 to order his attack delayed until sometime shortly after the appointed hour of 0400. Henry Roback of the *152d New York* described the haunting spectacle of the dawn, "A funeral silence pervades the assembly, and like specters the men in blue await the order to attack. At daylight the fog is heavy. Objects can only be seen four or five rods. An occasional musket shot can be heard in the distance, and a shell bounding down the hill..." The men in the ranks glumly awaited for the moment the fateful order to move out would be given. They had hardly any idea of what they were supposed to do, or what was expected of them. George Washburn of the *108th New York* wrote, "We knew nothing of what was before us, as this terrible night march had confused our ideas of direction, and we were so tired and bedraggled that we were reckless...." At 0435, Hancock finally

The high point of the battle of Spotsylvania, as envisioned in the North.

gave the order to attack and the powerful mass of thousands of bluecoated men stepped off up the sloping ground for the Confederate entrenchments.

The Federals first crossed a meandering brook to climb a hill swallowing up the unfortunate Confederate pickets located there. Continuing on, the Federal left encountered a smattering of picket fire causing Hancock to dispatch two of Gibbon's brigades, Owen's and Carroll's to protect it. The main charge continued on, going up a second hill where more pickets were encountered and sent running. During the charge, the organization of the attacking force began to fall apart with some soldiers turning the affair into a race by trying to outrun their comrades. From 100 to 150 yards away from the main line they encountered another depression containing abatis. Troops with axes hacked away while others clawed with their bare hands to move the obstruction; some even tried to crawl through. Onward they went, now encountering spotty fusillades from the Confederates in the salient. As B.F. Powellson of the *140th Pennsylvania*

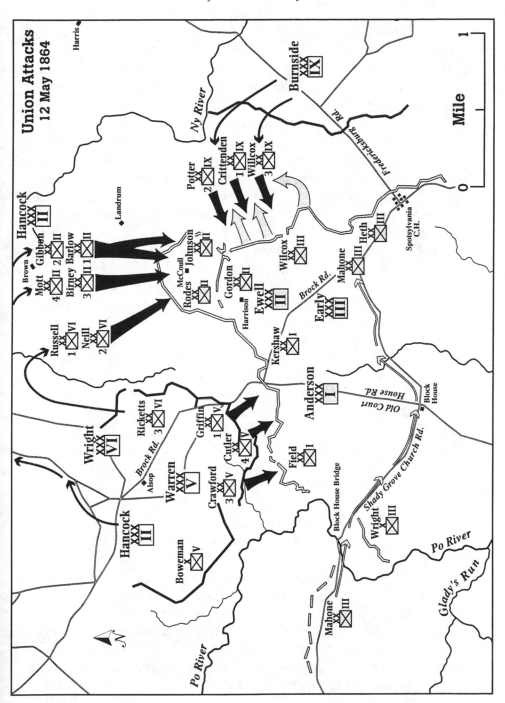

Union Attacks
12 May 1864

Mile

wrote, "The Rebels were taken by surprise, but there were enough of them to give us a warm reception."

Barlow's troops veered to the left in their charge to strike the enemy works head on, slamming into the Mule Shoe Salient nearly at its tip. Colonel Brooke recalled of the fighting to grab the trenches, "Never during the war have I seen such desperate fighting. The bayonet was freely used on both sides, the enemy fought desperately, and nothing but the formation of our attack and the desperate valor of our troops could have carried the point." An adjutant of the *126th New York* and his comrades had an easier time of it, "So surprised were they that some of their artillery men were killed in their works. Some were cooking, and some were asleep.... Within three minutes from the time we got into their works, we had their guns turned against them." A member of the *148th Pennsylvania* wrote that the Federals, "poured in like a great wave, driving out the Confederates pell mell with clubbed muskets and bayonets..." Barlow's men quickly overpowered York's Brigade capturing most of the Lousianians and sending those lucky enough to escape fleeing in a hasty retreat. William Carter's Virginia battery had the grave misfortune of returning to the salient just as the Federals were breaking through. The gunners only managed to get off a single shot before they heard the command, "Stop firing that gun." Carter, finding his command surrounded by Yankees musket barrels, yelled out, "Don't shoot my men!" and surrendered. Three guns under Lieutenant Charles R. Montgomery were also captured.

Once through, Barlow's Federals shifted slightly to the left, gobbling up Witcher's and then Steuart's brigades, which had been successfully fighting off the Federal forces in their front. Barlow's victorious Yankees swept on, reaching toward the rear of Lane's brigade, snapping up a couple of North Carolina regiments on his flank. Another Confederate battery under Reese was captured, though one gun did manage to get off the field to safety. New Yorker Henry Roback wrote of the near chaos amongst the Confederates, "The slaughter was fearful as we swept [the Confederates] from the field, and force them into

Confederate Generals Edward Johnson and George H. Steuart under guard behind Union lines.

our lines. They madly rush into their dugout shanty pits, piling up on each other, and through the intense excitement are shot, and writhe in agony." A Virginian in Witcher's Brigade had Federals within 30 feet of his position with others getting in the rear, causing one of his comrades to call out, "Stop firing, stop firing, they will kill all of us."

Birney's troops with Mott's command advanced on Barlow's right, contending with marshy and wooded ground, but managing to keep apace. Birney's formation rammed into the West Angle, gobbling up more of York's unfortunate Louisiana Brigade and eight cannon. The Yankee onslaught then slid to the right toward the southwest onto the flank of Walker's famed Stonewall Brigade, rolling up most of the elite Virginia regi-

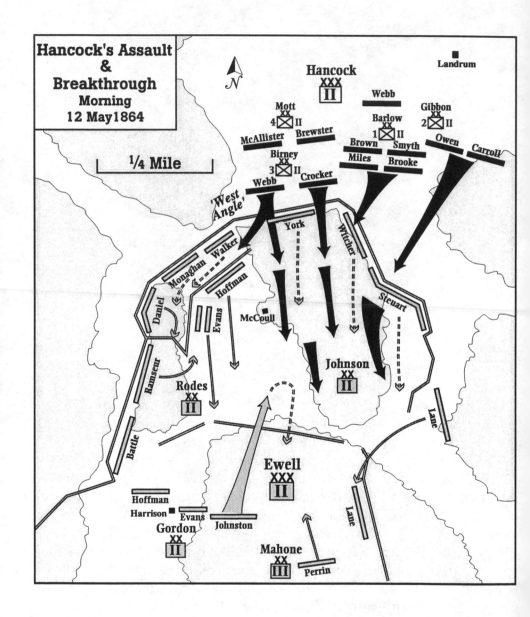

ments like a piece of paper. The next brigade under Junius Daniel had time to put troops on a line perpendicular with the main entrenchments and ably fought to protect the flank of Rodes' Division from the onslaught.

In control of the works, the Federals were exultant with victory. Washburne wrote, "The boys could not suppress their excessive joy any longer, but broke into a wild hurrah, which swept like a tempest from one end of the line to the other." In a little less than an hour a handsome catch had been made, nearly 3,000 prisoners, including division commander Johnson and brigade commander Steuart, were herded to the rear, 20 guns had been taken, and a gaping hole was left in the Confederate line. While a huge breakthrough had been won, there was still the danger that nothing might come from the initial success. Problems that had plagued Upton's advance two days before were now affecting the *II Corps'* drive. The formidable attacking column by now was a completely disorganized mass of men. Officers made some attempts at reorganization, but any success was beyond their efforts. Still, despite the confusion, the *II Corps* continued to press forward in the direction of Spotsylvania Court House with officers shouting, "Charge forward! To the interior line! We have them now! Up and at them! The Union forever! Hurrah, boys, hurrah." Some troops even tried to work the captured guns with one being fired at a 45 degree angle. When one of the novice cannoneers was told to depress the piece if he wanted to hit something, he responded, "Never fear: it's bound to come down on somebody's head." A jubilant Hancock was able to report to Meade, "Our men have the works, with some hundred prisoners; impossible to say how many; whole line moving up." Later, he was able to put a number on his captives, some 2,000 men including Johnson and Steuart. Meade replied, "Your good news is most welcome. Burnside at the appointed hour. Wright is ordered in at once on your right. Hold all you get and press on." The Confederate line may have been broken, but Lee had plenty of forces on hand to seal the breach. As one Federal said, "We thought we had captured the whole Rebel Army, but were not long in finding out our mistake."

The Federals continued their advance into the woods in the center of the salient, encountering an increasing volume of fire from the enemy that forced them to halt. Washburn of the *108th New York* related that at first the men responded professionally with musket fire of their own, "Our advance was not checked till our men had broken from the ranks, and could scarcely recognize each other each other in these thick woods, and so dense was the darkness that no attempt was made to keep a line, but each soldier acted upon his own responsibility, loading and firing at will." The intensity of musketry and cannon fire became furious as a *12th New Jersey* recalled, "Shells were bursting right in our faces with a report quicker and sharper than a lightning stroke, sending those rough, jagged, death-dealing fragments in all directions. The smell of powder and brimstone was almost suffocating, but on we rushed. At every step a life was lost—a man went down... The air was thick and hot with flashing, smoking, whirling missiles of death: the piteous, heartrending cries and groans of the wounded, and cheers and yells of defiance from the living." Yankee Roback said of the Rebel volleys inside the salient during the firefight, "...mowed down the boys like grain on the bloody field." Again Washburn wrote, "The rattle of musketry became so incessant that it was like peal after peal of thunder, long and continuous, vibrating up and down the great lines and echoing from front to rear. The dust and smoke from burnt wadding and powder was stifling. It hung like a pall over this field." All of a sudden, the attacking *II Corps* troops now found themselves the quarry of a surprise assault by counterattacking Confederate brigades that had been drawn from up and down Lee's line. Some Federals suddenly found themselves behind enemy ranks; a sergeant in the *141st Pennsylvania* did not realize Confederate soldiers were behind him until one put a hand on his shoulder and ordered him to drop his gun. Those who could ran for the rear and the trenches that had been carried earlier in the day. Once back at the main line, Colonel John Brooke found many soldiers who had not done their utmost; a large number of the *Third Division* stayed out of the fight to gather up spoils from abandoned

Confederate camps. But even here the Federals would not be safe, the enemy was coming to regain what had been lost and seal the hole that had been made in their line.

What had thrown the Federals back had not been a coordinated strike by a unified division or corps, instead it was a series of piecemeal attacks from a variety of commands that managed to be handy at the time of their army's greatest need. The first force to respond was the Confederate reserve, Gordon's Division of three brigades. John B. Gordon had withstood such a situation days before in the Wilderness where he broke apart a *V Corps* assault with a counterattack by his brigade. Now a division commander, he dispatched his brigades to the points where they were most needed. After 0530, Gordon sent one, R.D. Johnston's North Carolinians, toward the sound of fighting, their path taking them northeast into the wood behind the East Angle. The brigade fell into heavy combat with the enemy whose numbers were too powerful to fight off and the North Carolinians retreated after suffering heavy casualties including its commander. Gordon next committed half of Colonel Clement Evan's Georgians to stall the Yankees. Part of this command advanced to fight in the woods near the McCoull House to the point where they were nearly surrounded. Those who could tried to cut their way out to the rear while others were forced to surrender. Gordon set up a line of his remaining forces, the remnants of Evans' Brigade and Colonel John Hoffman's Brigade at the Harrison House where he would launch one more counterattack.

With Hoffman on the left and Evans on the right, Gordon's forces stepped off from the vicinity of the Harrison House heading northeast. Engaging the Yankees with the Rebel yell and fierce musketry, they forced them to stop and then retreat. Hoffman's Virginians chased them all the way back to the main works at the East Angle once held by Steuart's Brigade. Some of Hoffman's men even chased the Northerners over the works, but the brigade maintained its position in the retaken entrenchments. Lieutenant Colonel Christian of the 49th Virginia wrote about scurrying the Yankees off after taking the entrenchments,

The McCoull House, at the tip of the Confederate salient at Spotsylvania.

"...a little fire drove the enemy back into the cover of their pines. There was desultory fighting there all day though the enemy made no serious effort to carry the works again." The counter-attack of Hoffman's command also led to the recovery of four cannon and a couple of battle flags and the capture of a Union brigade commander, Colonel Hiram Brown. Evans' Georgia regiments did not repulse the enemy with the ease of Hoffman's men. Their attack had led them to stray to the south, leaving a flank open to enemy fire. The 61st Georgia there lost 65 men captured before it broke and fled for the rear. Despite this incident, the two remaining regiments advanced to recover the Confederate works south of Hoffman.

Other Confederate officers were also working hard to replug the gap. Ramseur's Brigade on the west face of the salient was pulled out of line, marched into the McCoull fields and faced north. While pushing northwards to bolster the beleaguered Daniel still holding a position in the salient, Ramseur was

Abner Perrin

wounded in the arm and taken from the field and his command devolved upon Colonel Bryan Grimes. Grimes continued the work, retaking the northwestern portion of the salient after the fire from his command sent the Federals fleeing for cover. More help was on the way in the form of Brigadier General Abner Perrin's Alabama Brigade from Mahone's Division on the Army of Northern Virginia's left. Perrin, new to the situation, halted his men near the Harrison House until he could find out what was going on. Meeting with Ewell, Rodes, and Gordon, the latter took responsibility for ordering the Alabama brigade into the fight. Perrin had his troops advance forward almost directly north across the McCoull Field. There they were caught in a maelstrom of fire and confusion, Perrin himself falling from his horse with a mortal wound. Only days before, he had told a comrade this battle would either lead to his death or a promotion. At the same time, Perrin's men caught fire from the rear

Troops of the **Union II Corps** *fight to hold on to Confederate rifle pits.*

which they assumed was from comrades mistaking the Alabamians for Federals. The Confederate colors were waved, but this only showed that the shots were indeed coming from Northerners retreating from Hoffman's attack. Still, the command advanced forward to take its part in retaking the works, advancing all the way to a position with Hoffman's men.

Over two hours after the *II Corps* had stepped off on their attack which had broken an entire Confederate division, Hancock's men had been nearly carried off the field by a series of ad hoc counterattacks by mere brigades. Meade would attempt to get Hancock's command to "push on" for much of the morning, only to have the corps commander complain his ranks were far too disorganized. He later told of being attacked by the enemy himself, but repulsing his advances. All Hancock could do now was to hold on to the part of the Confederate trenches seized in the early morning assault not yet retaken by the enemy, the very tip of the salient from the West Angle to just south of the East Angle. This space would become fiercely contested and literally soaked with blood.

Capture of Johnson and Steuart

After Hancock's divisions had pierced the Confederate salient at Spotsylvania, the scene at Grant's headquarters became hectic with activity and excited with news of a great victory. Couriers galloped into the camp, one after the other, with fresh reports, each one telling of great success on the battlefield. Staff-officers, standing around the camp's fire took time out from their work to give shouts and cheers with each happy account that the offensive was going well.

It was around 0630 that a strange sight suddenly appeared in camp, a mounted man in a Confederate officer's uniform splattered with mud, hair protruding from a hole in the crown of his felt hat. The man dismounted near the campfire and walked over to meet with Grant and Meade. Meade recognized the figure and took his hand warmly exclaiming, "Why how do you do, general?" Turning to Grant, the major general offered a formal introduction, "General Grant, this is General Johnson—Edward Johnson." Johnson was well known to officers of Grant's command: he had served at West Point with Major General Meade, fought in Mexico with Lieutenant General Grant, and had been a good acquaintance to staff officer Porter before the war. Grant extended pleasantries to Johnson who sadly replied, "I had not expected to meet you under such circumstances." A sympathetic Grant replied, "It is one of the many sad fortunes of war" and offered the captive a cigar and a seat next to the campfire. Johnson was soon comfortable and at ease despite his plight, talking convivially with both Grant and Meade. Another dispatch from Hancock arrived during the meeting with more exultant news of great battlefield success, "I have finished up Johnson and am now going into Early." In deference to his guest, Grant had the dispatch passed around rather than reading it aloud. Johnson finished his pleasant conversation and bid his guests good bye and proceeded to the rear. The general was subsequently exchanged and returned to active duty, seeing service with the Army of Tennessee.

The other noted captive of Hancock's 12 May breakthrough, Brigadier General George Steuart, enjoyed much less hospitality in Federal hands. Trapped hopelessly behind Union lines, he sought to give himself up with honor by surrendering to an enemy officer. He approached Colonel James Beaver of the *148th Pennsylvania* with this intent saying, "I would like to surrender to an officer of rank."

The obliging Beaver replied, "I would be very glad to receive your surrender sir; whom have I the honor to address."

"General Steuart."

Thinking he had a more illustrious captive, Beaver excitedly exclaimed, "What! Jeb Steuart?"

"No, George H. Steuart of the infantry."

The Federal colonel asked for

Steuart's sword who could only reply, "Well, sah, you all waked us up so early this mawnin' that I didn't get it on."

Beaver was still involved in the action on the field, so he could not personally direct Steuart to the rear, leaving that honor to a corporal. Steuart eventually made his way to Hancock's headquarters with a souring temperament from either his fate or the treatment by his new guard. At any rate, he was in an unfriendly mood to meet with the commander of the *II Corps*. When Hancock saw Steuart, he cordially offered his hand. The Confederate general drew back, saying, "Under the present circumstances, I must decline to take your hand." The offended Hancock shot back, "Under any other circumstances, general, I should not have offered it." Hancock had given Johnson the horse he used to ride to Grant's camp, but this unhappy exchange cooled his generosity. He let Steuart make his way to the rear on foot.

CHAPTER VII

"One Continuous Roll of Musketry"

12 May 1864

News of Hancock's breakthrough reached Grant's headquarters around 0530 followed by reports of further successes. While members of the general's staff received the good tidings with much exultation, Grant himself remained reserved, in Porter's words, "...giving his constant thoughts to devising methods for making victory complete." Only when he was told of the *II Corps'* huge captures did he show any noticeable excitement. "That's the kind of news I like to hear. I had hoped that a bold dash at daylight would secure a number of prisoners. Hancock is doing well." Hancock also asked for reinforcements, but Grant had already detailed the *VI Corps* to go to his aid.

At 0600 Wright was ordered to move Neill's and Rickett's divisions of the *VI Corps* toward the action. The fighting almost proved too much for the corps commander when he received a mild wound from a shell shortly after receiving Grant's directions. Fortunately, the injury was not serious enough to force Wright to leave the field and miss seeing his troops go into action.

First to enter the fray for the *VI Corps* was Colonel Oliver Edward's *Fourth Brigade* of Neill's division. This moved up to form a line with its left connecting with Mott's troops and the right extending to the West Angle where they found the opportunity to fire on the right flank of Ramseur's Confederates. Two other brigades of Neill's came on the field, going into position behind Edwards men, Colonel Daniel Bidwell's *Third Brigade* and Brigadier Frank Wheaton's *First Brigade*. Colonel Wheaton said of his troops' position, "Here we were exposed to the most terrible musketry fire, losing heavily, including many valuable officers." The last of Neill's brigades, Brigadier General Lewis A. Grant's hard-fighting Vermonters, marched to relieve Barlow's exhausted division. The brigade went into position on the far left of the *II Corps* in front of the Confederate works while suffering from a "terrible" fire.

The Confederates were receiving reinforcements as well. Brigadier General Nathaniel Harris' Brigade of Mahone's Division had marched up to participate in the fight at the works around 0730. Harris himself was a University of Louisiana law graduate who had climbed through the ranks into general command after raising a company of infantry early in the war. With battle experience and distinction from Williamsburg through Gettysburg, he was the right man to have on the scene at a moment of great need. The fight at the Mule Shoe was just such a time, as Ramseur's Brigade was just about to break from enemy fire and Harris' Mississippians were trying to avert that possibility by taking position on their right. Getting to Ramseur's flank proved to be a difficult problem. Harris' men were suffering from the Yankee fire and his guide either had left the scene or had been killed or wounded. After finding a soldier who could give him directions, Harris' Brigade charged forward toward Ramseur's position, suffering heavy casualties while forcing back Yankees of the *Excelsior Brigade* of Mott's division through fierce hand-to-hand combat. With the *Excelsior Brigade* forced to retreat, some of Ramseur's troops could get into the woods north of the entrenchments on the right of Edwards' *Fourth Brigade*. From this advantageous position, they trained their fire on the unfortunate *10th Massachusetts*. Low on ammunition, the Massachusetts regiment had to fall back. The next regiment in line, the *2nd Rhode Island*, swung its right flank back to connect with the Bay Staters in their new recessed position.

More Confederate reinforcements were on the way. Another Southern brigade, Brigadier General Samuel McGowan's command of South Carolinians from Wilcox's Division, arrived from the Army of Northern Virginia's right. On the advance to the main entrenchments, starting around 0900, McGowan's Brigade found itself in a tempest of fire from the front and the flank. Colonel Joseph Brown of the brigade's 14th South Carolina recorded of the advance, "The charge was made facing a terrific fire in front and a more terrific fire from the enemy in the right of the Angle. It is only a soldier familiar with battle that knows the fatal effect of a flank fire." The effects of the fire were especially telling on the commanders of the brigade: McGowan was struck down with a wound and the next ranking officer, Colonel B.T. Brockman, was mortally wounded. Colonel Charles McCreary and Lieutenant Colonel W.P. Shooter of the 1st South Carolina also fell with wounds as did Colonel Mill of Orr's Rifles. In the resulting confusion, Lieutenant Colonel Isaac F. Hunt of the 13th South Carolina understandably thought himself the ranking officer in the thick of the fight and took temporary control of the brigade advancing it all the way to Harris' right behind the West Angle, leaving behind a substantial number of casualties in the wake of the advance. The arrival of the surviving South Carolinians made the situation too hot for the *2nd Rhode Island* and *10th Massachusetts*, both of which retreated from the front line. However, the retreat of these Yankees did not mean the battle was over for the men of McGowan's Brigade. For the next 17 hours its troops would be under what one of its officers would call "...the most terrible rain of minnie balls recorded in the history of warfare."

Sometime just before 0930, the second of Wright's *VI Corps* divisions under Russell arrived to do battle. The lead brigade was headed by Emory Upton, the Union hero of the successful attack on the Mule Shoe just two days earlier. His men occupied a crest overlooking the works on the right of Edward's brigade just as its right was cracking. The first of Upton's regiments to

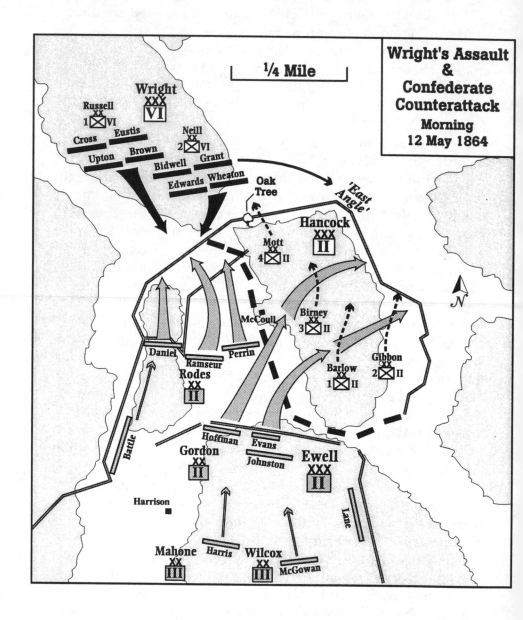

This view of the Bloody Angle at Spotsylvania, seen from the Union side, shows vividly the driving rain in which parts of the battle were fought.

reach the field was the *95th Pennsylvania* which took horrible casualties while taking the crest and making a line from in front of the West Angle extending west. A soldier with the regiment wrote, "I cannot imagine how any of us survived the sharp fire that swept over us at this point—a fire so keen that it split the blades of grass all about us, the minies moaning in a furious concert as they picked out victims by the score." Despite the maelstrom of fire, Upton urged the men on, yelling out, "hold this ground." The rest of Upton's brigade took up position, getting into a heavy firefight with the Confederate troops only 300 yards away.

As if the awful storm of fire was not enough to torment the embattled troops, the sky let loose with a terrific rain upon the bloodied field. The downpour did nothing to cool the fighting temperament of the youthful Upton, no doubt self-impressed with his recent field promotion to brigadier general. He rode up to Lieutenant Colonel Joseph Parsons of the *10th Massachusetts* at 1000, dressed in a cavalry overcoat, with the intention of having the unit move closer to the enemy trenches. Dismounting, he asked who was in charge of the regiment. Parsons replied he was in command only to have the newcomer boldly proclaim, "This is no position for this regiment. Swing this regiment over the slope up against the works." When the colonel tried to explain his position, he received an impatient rebuke, "I want no explanation from you, sir. I am General Upton; I order it done at once." Parsons refused, writing later, "I had been in the service long enough to know that I had a brigade commander and a division commander and would not take orders from any outsider at such a time as this, unless I agreed thoroughly with him." The outraged Upton threatened a court-martial for this disobedience. When this did not win compliance, he stormed off, returning to ask who was in charge of the brigade and was told brigade commander Eustis was away getting troops, leaving Colonel Edwards in command. Upton left once more and returned with Edwards, himself, who said, "This is General Upton; he ranks me and he orders you to swing your troops against the works." Parsons replied, "Colonel Edwards, you are in command of the Brigade. My advice to you is that you give Upton the same answer that I did." While this conversation was going on a column of troops appeared. Upton said, "I will take these new troops and will show you how soon these works can be taken and held." Indeed, Upton took command of the oncoming regiments and brashly ordered them forth in assaults against the works. Parsons wrote of their fate, "He ordered the first regiment to charge up over the slope up against the works. They received a tremendous fire as they came up out of the ravine on the front and flank. No troops could stand such a fire and they were driven back in confusion, leaving the ground strewn with their dead and wounded. He then ordered the second regiment with the same result." Upton then came to Edwards and said, "Troops cannot live over that slope; I have ordered the other regiment to report to you and I advise that the line be extended from your right around the knoll."

The Federal attempts to hold against the terrific fire was an ordeal that required bravery, willpower and a healthy supply of ammunition, as the men of Colonel Brooke's brigade of Barlow's *II Corps* division found out. Brigadier General Wheaton called upon Brooke's command, resting and reorganizing at the Landrum House, to advance and guard his right flank. Brooke protested that Hancock had asked his command to support the *VI Corps* and not go in to battle unless it was "to save the day." Wheaton insisted and Brooke's 1,000 men went forward to fight until their ammunition was exhausted, forcing men to go to the rear with caps and blankets to collect cartridges. Brooke asked to be relieved and his command was pulled out.

Despite the fire, some Yankee commands tried desperate attacks against the blazing enemy line. One of Bidwell's regiments charged against the Rebel entrenchments at the West Angle, but was driven back. At 1000, Brown's *New Jersey Brigade* arrived and went forward against Ramseur's and Harris' position. They Garden State Yankees made it to the entrenchments at the cost of 200 men and managed to get into the works for a few moments before being thrust out and losing 110 more men. The troops lucky enough to return from the action unscathed were then taken out of the battle and committed to the reserve.

Deciding to bring some artillery to bear on the Confederates, the ubiquitous Emory Upton sent a staff officer to have a nearby battery, *Battery C of the 5th U.S. Artillery* send a section for his use. The commander of the guns, First Lieutenant James Gillis at first refused Upton's lieutenant, only to have the man return with an officer of higher rank who ordered Gillis to obey. In obedience, Gillis sent Second Lieutenant Richard Metcalf's two guns into the blistering combat. These unlimbered near Upton and attracted the attention of some of Harris' men who surged forward in an attempt to take them. Against this threat, Metcalf's guns belched forth swaths of canister, mowing down the attackers. The battle was now raging at what was described as "white heat," but regardless, Metcalf's guns were pushed forward even closer to the enemy line. Soon the fire was so intense the pieces had to be abandoned, leaving behind the bodies of most of the artillerists that had taken them into action. Metcalf's section had gone in with 23 men and 1 officer. His engagement had left all of the horses of his section killed, 7 of his men dead and 16 wounded. A testament to the intensity of fire was that the gun carriages were so butchered by bullets, they were now entirely unusable. Other guns from the *II Corps* artillery were set up in a comparatively safer position north of the salient on the Landrum house lane where they bellowed a destructive rain of shot and shell on the enemy position. Some guns were advanced closer to the Confederate defenders to deliver loads of canister and were pulled back once their supplies of this ammunition were exhausted.

The most intense part of the conflagration on the Confederate side was the right of McGowan's Brigade. Colonel Brown of the 14th South Carolina had now taken command from Lieutenant Colonel Hunt, but kept the troops under a dual command structure. Brown oversaw his troops near the right of his line while he kept Hunt in an instrumental role of forwarding troops and ammunition from the left to the more heavily engaged troops on the right. As soldiers on the right fell, the ranks on the other flank of Brown's Brigade ran to take their places. Reinforcements were also appropriated from Harris' Brigade on Brown's left. That force had lost so many officers that many enlisted men were soon left fighting under their own direction. Help was also sought from Ramseur's Brigade, but word came back that this force could not be weakened. The desperate situation led to some critical moments as when some soldiers of the *26th Michigan* and *61st New York* crawled forward through the muck and carnage around 1200 to assail Brown's Rebels near the West Angle opposite the Oak Tree. Once close enough, the Yankees suddenly leaped up, fired, and charged into the works fighting with bayonets and clubbed muskets. Brown's men forced the interlopers out of the works, but they remained near enough to engage in a firefight at close range.

On the other side of the field, probably no brigade on the Federal side had a tougher time of it than Edwards' command. The arrival of Eustis' brigade in the afternoon prompted Colonel

Edwards to request an attack of that brigade, Upton's and Bidwell's to relieve his own force, finding that it could not be done since there was too much confusion in their rank to make such an assault effective. At 1600, the fire had slackened enough to allow *II Corps* troops to take the place of Colonel Edwards' Massachusetts and Rhode Island troops while they retreated about 30 yards to the rear. Edwards asked division commander Neill if he couldn't have his brigade totally relieved, but the answer was no; Edwards had to stay in position to allow Upton's and Bidwell's brigades to pull back after dark. To ameliorate the situation of Edwards, General Russell offered the *10th New Jersey* in as a reinforcement. At 1800, the *II Corps* troops that had relieved them left their position, forcing Edwards' men up once again to their old position in the thick of the fire. Increasingly frustrated, Edwards threatened another *II Corps* brigade commander at gunpoint for attempting to remove his brigade from its supporting position.

Throughout the late morning and afternoon the fighting at the salient remained so intense, particularly at the point where Grant's, Upton's and Edward's men were so close to the Confederate line, that the opposing forces were firing literally into each others' faces. Hundreds of rounds were expended as the fusillades continued and muskets became so fouled men had to fall out of the ranks to clean them. Other Federal attacks took place at soldier's own initiative with men crawling forward to the enemy entrenchments with a fence rail or piece of abatis to throw over the top. A few soldiers went as far as to jump up on the trenches and fire musket after musket handed to them until shot down by enemy fire. When the opportunity arose, the bayonet or musket butt was employed. Captain F.H. Barney of the *5th Vermont* recalled, "The engagement... resembled a hand-to-hand fight rather than a modern battle with long-range weapons. The men clubbed their muskets, and repelled repeated advances by mere physical force." Private James E. Wilson of the *10th Massachusetts* got captured by Confederates and was sent to the rear where he found himself exposed to a hurricane of bullets. With the fire so dangerous, he tried to wait out the battle behind the breastworks only to be ejected by some Rebels who wanted his cover. He then tried to take shelter behind a stump a couple of rods to the rear, hugging the ground dearly to avoid the deadly missiles in the air about him. During a truce Wilson was able to break to Union lines, but not before seeing that the position he had been forced to leave was now full of enemy dead. Sergeant Sidney Williams of the same regiment and three of his comrades were forced to find cover in captured rifle pits, a decision he later regretted, "This was a very unfortunate move" since the men found themselves in what seemed a "hornet's nest of fire." One of Williams' comrades was killed trying to get back to the regiment, another was killed by a bullet to the heart and died "without a struggle, like a child going to sleep." The other member managed to escape while Williams was taken into Confederate lines as a prisoner.

The rain, cold and drenching, continued to pour on the field throughout the day, adding a special grimness to the horrific spectacle of death. A member of the *Philadelphia Brigade* wrote:

> The most sanguinary and deadly fight of this campaign began at this moment. During the entire day and far into the night there was one continuous roll of musketry. Repeated charges were made by the enemy, only to be as frequently repulsed. Occasionally both Union and Confederate flags were on the breastworks at the same moment, and for the time the concentration of fire told with fearful effect. The most desperate contest was about the salient, and in front of it the sight was one of horror. Those killed in the charge at daylight lay before the works, while every repulse of Confederates left an increased number, until bodies were lying across each other in heaps. The fire was so incessant that the dead were repeatedly struck with balls from both sides, and the wounded in many cases perished before the sun went down on the scene of blood.

Adjutant Muffley of the *148th Pennsylvania* wrote:

> Words can give no adequate idea of the dreadful sanguinary conflict. Hour after hour, all day long men grappled over the works in bloody struggle. They fired guns full in each other's

faces. They lunged at each other with bayonet thrust. They leaped upon the works and fired down among the maddened crowd on the other side. They grappled in mortal combat to wrest flags from each other. They held their guns overhead and shot downward into the enemy. Hour after hour, all day long, they fought like demons. It was a literal saturnalia of blood. It was a grim visaged full panoply of horror. All day long the rain fell and the ground was mingled with blood and water.

Henry George with the *139th Pennsylvania* wrote:

Wild cheers, savage yells and frantic shrieks rose above the sighing of the wind, and the spattering of the rain and formed a demoniacal accompaniment to the booming guns of the guns as they hurled their missiles of death into the contending ranks.

On the Confederate side, descriptions of the combat were just as bleak. Colonel Brown related, "It was a rainy day and water stood in the trenches, reddened with the blood of our wounded and dead comrades, and before dark the dead were so thick in the traverses toward the right that the living had not standing room without trampling on them, and they laid them in heaps to make room." The fire was enough to make a Confederate doctor behind the lines extremely nervous about what was going on at the front. He wrote home in a letter, "The musketry and cannon continued from daybreak until night. Nothing that I have ever before heard compared with it... Such musketry I never heard before and it continued all night... It was perfectly fearful. I never experienced such an anxiety in my life. It was an awful day, and it seemed to me as if all the 'Furies of Darkness' had come together in combat. Everybody who was not firing was pale with anxiety, but our noble soldiers stood their ground, fighting with utmost desperation."

Increasingly, there appeared little more that the Union forces could do at the tip of the salient than hold on to the yards of trenches which had not been reoccupied by Confederate troops. If a success was to be had, it would be reliant on the activities of the two remaining corps of the *Army of the Potomac*.

Horatio Wright

Born in Clinton, Connecticut on 6 March 1820, Wright graduated from West Point an admirable second in a class containing a sizable number of Civil War comrades and enemies including John Reynolds, Nathaniel Lyon, Don Carlos Buell and Richard Garnett. His years after graduation were occupied with engineering projects with the *Corps of Engineers* including the construction of harbors and fortifications. He was also a teacher of French and engineering at the Military Academy.

Wright was wrapped up in the drama of the Civil War during its earliest days. When Virginia left the Union after Fort Sumter, Wright was chief engineer of an expedition sent to reinforce the Norfolk Navy Yard where a large flotilla of ships was kept, including the USS *Merrimac* (later the CSS *Virginia*). Wright was captured during the operation, but was released in time to serve at First Bull Run as brigade commander Colonel Samuel Heintzelman's chief engineer.

For the first two years of the war Wright served first in operations on the South Carolina coast and then in the *Department of Ohio* before getting a command of a division under *VI Corps* commander John Sedgwick and fighting at Gettysburg, Mine Run, and the Wilderness. When Sedgwick was killed at Spotsylvania on 9 May, Wright was appointed to take command of the corps. Under Wright's direction the *VI Corps* fought with Grant for the rest of the

offensive that would take the *Army of the Potomac* to Petersburg. However, Wright would not remain as part of the siege. Jubal Early's Washington Raid caused Grant to send the *VI Corps* to defend the Union capital against the enemy force that was bearing down on the city. He then took his troops into the Shenandoah Valley during Sheridan's famous offensive through the fertile region. He fought under Sheridan in the Union victories of Winchester (19 September 1864) and Fisher's Hill (22 September 1864) against Jubal Early. On 19 October, while Sheridan was away from the field, Wright was in command of the Federal army when it was attacked and routed by a surprise attack from Early. Wright was instrumental in saving the day by rallying the broken forces which Sheridan then led back into battle to win a complete victory. When Sheridan's mission in the valley was completed, Wright and the *VI Corp* returned to service with the *Army of the Potomac* fighting in the last battles of the war.

After the war, Wright continued in the military at a Regular Army rank of lieutenant colonel with command over the *Department of Texas*. He rose in the ranks of the Regulars eventually attaining a brigadier generalship and the post of chief engineer working on several projects including the Washington Monument. Wright retired in 1884 and died 15 years later.

CHAPTER VIII

Attack at All Hazards

12 May 1864

*U*nfortunately for the Union, neither Burnside's *IX Corps* nor Warren's *V Corps* pursued their participation in the battle with much vigor. Both probed and skirmished, but the major attacks that might have broken the enemy line or at least diverted Confederate troops from joining the fighting going on at the salient never came.

Burnside himself had his troops on the move at 0400 with Potter's division in the van followed by the *First Division*, now under Major General Thomas L. Crittendon, while the remaining division, under Willcox, remained in reserve. The *IX Corps* advanced against the position of Lane's Brigade, netting some prisoners, entrenchments and a couple of artillery pieces. For a short time, a connection was made with the *II Corps*, the junction being held by the *9th New Hampshire*, which turned out to be in a rather dangerous spot. A staff officer rode up to the commander of the New Hampshire unit, Major Chandler, urgently shouting, "For God's sakes, major, change front and come to our left—they are flanking us!" Chandler was unsure what to do, but gave the necessary order. His troops advanced only a short distance before they found a large number of Confederates. The enemy troops and the New Hampshire men started firing at each other with the Federals taking the worst of it. Major Chandler had turned to his comrade Captain Copp and said, "Copp, this is tough going isn't it? We shall have to get out!" The *9th New Hampshire* then scurried for cover under the call, "every man for himself!" During the retreat, Copp saw the color bearer lying on the ground upon his flag. Thinking he might be waiting to surrender, Copp gave him a swift kick telling him to get up. The soldier responded, "Captain, I can't; I'm hit." Seeing it was true, Copp took the colors and ran after his retreating men shouting, "Rally on the colors boys!" Copp rallied about 70 of them and had them start firing. The damp weather ruined the powder of some charges and only half of the rifles would go off and some men threw away their guns in disgust. Copp recounted that he had never heard so much swearing in his life. Also wounded during the retreat was the unfortunate Major Chandler, who had to be carried from the field.

The Confederates began to engage the rest of Potter's command, including an attempt to turn his left where the *36th Massachusetts* held ground. At first the Rebels maneuvering against the Bay Staters were thought to be some of those Southerners captured by Hancock's men, and a captain yelled, "No, don't fire!" But enemy fusillades soon displayed the truth that these were attackers, not subdued captives. While Potter's left was under some pressure for some time, the enemy was beaten off.

The Federals dug in and let the morning pass, despite repeated orders coming from Grant to Burnside and the lieutenant general's observer on the scene, Lieutenant Colonel Cyrus Comstock, to press an attack and link up with the *II Corps*. After 0545, Grant sent a message with news of Hancock's success urging Burnside to "push on with all vigor." At 0800, he advised the *IX Corps* commander to link up with Hancock by pressing forward. Nearly an hour and a half later, Grant told Burnside to have one division link up with Hancock while the other two advanced against the enemy. Burnside evidently was not easily moved to activity and held his ground.

Meanwhile a spattering fire was kept up between the lines

throughout the morning, though with the smoke and fog hovering over the battlefield, it was nearly impossible for the troops to know if they were actually hitting anything. During the morning, Lyman Jackman, a soldier in the *6th New Hampshire* had two close calls. He found his original cover of a sapling pine insufficient to provide comfortable protection from bullets flying "as thick as hail." When he moved to a safer position, another soldier took his place and was soon struck down dead with a bullet in the head. Moving again, a soldier from the *48th Pennsylvania* this time came up to take his place. Despite the firefight, the Pennsylvanian fell asleep with his chin resting on folded arms. Jackman saw what happened next, "...while the writer was looking at him, and thinking how weary he must be to go to sleep in such a dangerous place, a minie ball struck the sleeper just above the right temple, his life blood streamed out upon the grass, and without opening up his eyes or moving hand or foot, he was dead."

After 1020, Burnside decided to follow Grant's orders to link up with the *II Corps* and attack, the *Third Division* under Willcox being directed to accomplish the task. The impact of the move was lost in an embarrassing spectacle of dithering confusion. At first Willcox was dispatched to the right to assist Hancock, but this order was countermanded. Around 1400, the division was assigned the task of attacking from Crittendon's left. Willcox was unsure about the wisdom of doing so since the enemy appeared at the moment ready to attack him. The order stood, nonetheless, and some action had to be taken. With Colonel John J. Hartranft's *First Brigade* in the lead, Willcox's troops moved forward into a wood in front of the Confederate works, before a bulge or salient in their line occupied by troops of Heth's Division. Willcox's premonition of an enemy attack proved correct for as he moved forward to assault, his force ran into a Confederate attack aimed at rolling up Burnside's flank.

These troops were of Heth's and Wilcox's Confederate divisions which opposed Burnside on the west side of the salient. One of Wilcox's brigade commanders, Brigadier General James Lane, had sent skirmishers to the east to probe the enemy's

David A. Weisinger, later to
win distinction at Petersburg.

position. Finding Burnside's left flank was hanging without any protection, Lane decided to advance and turn it. The diminutive Lane, called the "Little General" by his troops, had led his command of North Carolinians through some tight spots before, including Pickett's Charge at Gettysburg where it lost half its number. Lane's troops moved off at 1400, with Colonel David Weisiger leading Mahone's Brigade in support, into the woods not far to the southeast from the bulge in the Confederate line roughly about the same time Willcox had stepped off on his attack. Heading to the north, the Confederates first engaged some Union artillery which they nearly crippled with rifle fire. Help from nearby infantry regiments allowed the cannons to remain in action and devastate the enemy with blasts of grapeshot and canister. This deadly combination was enough to force Lane's men to retreat into the woods after suffering significant casualties.

Undaunted, Lane headed his men northwest where they fell upon the flank of Willcox's advance held by Colonel John F. Hartranft's *First Brigade*. The collision was nearly disastrous for the Federals. The *17th Michigan* was wrapped up in the Confederate attack, most of its men falling prey to their advance and being captured. The next regiment in line, the *51st Pennsylvania*, was sent fleeing to the rear. The *50th Pennsylvania* and *21st Michigan* of the brigade supporting Hartranft was also sent into retreat after having to cut their way to the rear, leaving many men as prisoners. A soldier of the *50th Pennsylvania* reported of the encounter, "The bayonet and butt end of the muskets were freely used." Sergeant James Levan of the same regiment learned that his unit was almost surrounded when he was confronted by a huge Confederate waving a sword who bellowed, "Surrender, you Yank, its all up with you." Levan decided to make for the rear with his comrades rather than obey the order. The *1st Michigan Sharpshooters* and the *27th Michigan* got pinned down behind a breastwork only 50 yards in front of the salient, a position they held at the cost of 300 men. With Willcox's division hastening to the rear, Lane could have pressed forward for further success, only his support failed to help and the brigade had to fall back to its trenches. Lee and Early tried to follow up this success with another attack from Heth's salient, this time with Weisiger's and Cooke's Brigades. The Federals were now entrenched by this time and the resulting attack was unable to accomplish any great success.

Burnside had failed to act or attack to his utmost on the eastern face of the salient and Warren's performance on the western face was similar, if not more lackluster and obdurate. As early as 0600, Warren had been ordered to be ready to advance and support Hancock's forces already engaged. Over an hour and a half later, Warren received a dispatch from Meade telling him Hancock was involved in heavy fighting with the Confederates and could be helped by an immediate attack. Troops were requested for the left flank to bolster Wright's *VI Corps* in case it found the fighting too much, a request that was amplified by a message from the *VI Corps* commander himself asking for troops to strengthen his right flank. Warren responded by sending most of Brigadier General Joseph Bartlett's brigade and Colonel J. Howard Kitching's *Heavy Artillery* brigade. Still, the high command was eager for a more aggressive act by the *V Corps* and orders from the lieutenant general of all the armies worked their way through the pipeline to the corps commander. At 0800, Grant ordered Meade to have Warren attack with as many troops as he could spare. Warren replied he had issued orders to attack, but complained that not enough time had been given to assault key points, including one position in the front of the *VI Corps* where enemy fire was enfilading his line and even getting into his rear. Indeed, a halfhearted attack was underway at 0815 and while the Federals managed to get within 50 yards of the enemy line held by Bratton's Brigade, the assault collapsed under heavy musketry.

This led Warren to send two discouraging missives to an increasingly disapproving Meade at 0910. In one, Warren requested Bartlett's command back to assist his division under Griffin. Worse though was the corps commander's statement, "I cannot advance my men at present." In the second 0910 message, Warren elaborated on the *V Corps*'s difficulty, reporting that his left could not attack until the *VI Corps* broke through its front because of enemy's flanking fire on the *V Corps* left. Another problem was the fact that his right was close to the enemy's position which was very strongly held. An angry Meade had his chief of staff A.A. Humphreys send Warren orders to attack immediately at 0915, "The order of the major-general commanding is peremptory that you attack at once at all hazards with your whole force if necessary." Two messages followed, both dated fifteen minutes later, that seemed a bit more conciliatory. In one Humphreys told Warren, "Don't hesitate to attack with the bayonet. Meade has assumed the responsibility and will take the consequences." and signed it "your friend." The corps commander was then placated with news that Bartlett's brigade would be returned to him and with an announcement that since the *II Corps* and *VI Corps* were heavily engaged, it was unlikely that the enemy facing the *V Corps* could be all that strong. Warren received the directive by 0930 and gave the necessary orders to his subordinates to carry out its instructions. He reported to Humphreys at 0940, "My orders are to attack with bayonet without regard to consequences that may result unfavorably." This Meade took as an indication that Warren was not too hopeful that his attack would succeed. If that was indeed the case, Warren was told to prepare to have his troops sent to support Wright and Hancock.

Moving forward in the *V Corps* attack were elements of Colonel Jacob Swietzer's and Brigadier General Roman Ayres' brigades of Griffin's division, and Cutler's division. Griffin's division swept forward across a field of swells and depressions only to get cut down by fire from Bratton's and Dubose's Brigades. The attack fell apart with men taking whatever cover they could find. Confederate colonel Bratton recorded of the assault, "the enemy assaulted us heavily, advancing beautifully in two lines of battle. We held our fire to within 50 yards of us, when by a deliberate and well directed volley a line of their dead was laid down across the entire front of my brigade excepting one regiment.... The fusillade continued for some minutes and strewed the field with dead and wounded from their scattered and fleeing hordes."

Cutler's division surged forward against Law's command in three lines, the crack *Iron Brigade* in the lead followed by Bragg's and Lyle's brigades. The first two commands made it to the abatis in front of the Confederate line where they suffered from canister and musketry. The incredible valor of the assaulting columns was cheapened when Cutler told Warren his men could not advance any farther, only to get a response from the commander to put his situation in writing so it could be given to Meade. Colonel William C. Oates, a witness in the Confederate ranks, wrote of the Federal attack "...well fortified with head logs, our men but little exposed, and our fire so destructive that the enemy could not face it for long."

On Cutler's right, Crawford's *Pennsylvania Reserves* advanced against G.T. Anderson's and John Gregg's Confederate Brigades, though with the Keystone Staters' enlistments almost up, they were not about to sacrifice their lives with a trip home to safety looming on the near horizon. They probed Confederate positions, but did not do much more.

Warren had told his superiors that his troops had been ordered to attack with the bayonet without regard for the consequences of the rashness of the attack. The *V Corps* troops never even got close enough to do anything more than fire a rifle shot. At 1030, an hour after the attack had been launched, Warren admitted defeat. This only exasperated the frustrated Grant, who was becoming increasingly impatient with his *V Corps* commander, to the point of telling Meade at 1040 that the general was to be relieved and replaced by Humphreys if he did not make an attack. Grant spoke of his diminishing confidence in Warren to his staff officers, "I feel sorry to be obliged to send such an order in regard to Warren. He is an officer for whom I had conceived a very high regard. His quickness of perception, personal gallantry, and soldierly bearing pleased me, and a few days ago I should have been inclined to place him in command of the Army of the Potomac in case Meade had been killed; but I began to feel, after his want of vigor on the 8th, that he was not as efficient as I had believed, and his delay in attacking and the feeble character of his assaults to-day confirm me in my apprehensions." While Meade agreed with Grant's decision and had also come to have little faith in the success of Warren's 0930 attack, he allowed the commander of the *V Corps* to remain in command. Porter said of Warren's actions during the morning of 12 May, "Although the instructions were of the most positive and urgent character, he did not accomplish the work expected of him."

Warren's direction for the rest of the battle was to contract his lines and dispatch his forces to assist the *II Corps* and *VI Corps*. Cutler's division was the first to march, its mission being to reinforce the embattled Wright. Griffin's division was ordered to make for Hancock's lines where it went into a supporting position. Smoke obscured the field, but there were cheers from the *II Corps* at the sight of reinforcements. Cutler's division arrived at the *VI Corps'* position in the early afternoon, its troops reinforcing that unit's line. The new arrivals settled down to shoulder arms in the already gruesome slugfest. A member of the *24th Michigan* told of his regiments part in that fight,

"Standing in deep mud and keeping up a constant fire for hours... the men's muskets became so foul that details were made to clean the guns while their comrades kept up the fire. The men were so weary (having been under fire night and day for a week), that some lay down in the mud under the enemy's fire and slept soundly amid the thunder of battle, despite all efforts to arrouse them." While the rest of Warren's troops joined the fight, Crawford's division was to remain in a defensive position with the *Maryland Brigade* and the *V Corps* artillery.

While the fighting continued, commanders on both sides made dispositions for the results of the bleak day. During the afternoon, Lee had come to the conclusion that, even despite his reluctance to allow his line to be broken, he would not be able to drive the enemy entirely away from the salient. As a result, the position would have to be abandoned in favor of a new line 1,200 yards to the rear where a new line had already been begun. Survivors of Johnson's Division, artillerymen, and stragglers rounded up by the provost marshall's troops built the new line throughout the day. Unfortunately, the forces battling away at the salient wouldn't be able to fall back to this new position until cover of darkness and thus would have to remain in combat for the time being. Warren's inactivity during the afternoon gave Lee the opportunity to send reinforcements to areas of need as Humphreys' and Bratton's brigades were drawn from the First Corps lines and sent into position at the reserve entrenchments.

Despite the need to withdraw from the Mule Shoe, heartening word was spreading through the Southern ranks. Confident the position at Spotsylvania was going to be maintained despite the earlier breakthrough and the day's hard fighting, Confederate troops communicated the encouraging news up and down on the Confederate line. Soldiers called out to their comrades as the afternoon hours ticked by, "All right on the right" and "We've had a desperate time of it in the center, but we're not whipped to hurt." The effect was positive on members of the Texas Brigade, but there was the ever present reminder of the cost of the battle. A soldier of the Lone Star State wrote, "While such reports came and we received them exultingly, behind them, in cases where the fighting had been severe, we could hear the groans of the wounded and dying, and in the light of our own experiences, the fast stiffening bodies of the slain."

As determination strengthened the resolve of Confederate ranks, their numerically superior enemy counterparts were to becoming numbed by anxiety as Federal commanders readjusted their lines in fear of a Southern counterattack. At 1745, Hancock was warned about the continued gap between his own and Burnside's line along with the possibility that the enemy might try to exploit it. A quarter of an hour later, Hancock was ordered to strengthen his line as much as possible while maintaining a reserve which might be used with the *II Corps* or any other part of the line that might need it. There had been hopes that Wright might be able to press and attack with Warren's reinforcements, but the *VI Corps* commander told his superiors throughout the afternoon that even with the reinforcements, he could not renew the assault. At 1815, Meade gave his approval of that decision. Instead of being aggressive, Wright pleaded with Warren for more of his troops to replace his own battle weary brigades. These appeals fell on the deaf ears of the *V Corps* commander, who was not willing to risk having his forces fiercely engaged since they had seen battle during the day as well and were quite weary. There was also the ever present worry that the enemy might launch a counterattack, so the *V Corps'* strength might aid the entire army if its strength was conserved.

Fear of an enemy attack also existed on the Federal left. There was concern throughout the night that Burnside might be attacked and he was warned about the possibility and at 1810 he was told to strengthen his line. Nearly three hours later Grant asked him to remain alert early the next morning to meet an expected enemy attack. As a result of such timidity, there were no plans for active Federal operations on the 13th.

The evening fears of potential enemy attacks did not dissuade Grant from giving Halleck a positive spin on the day's fighting, claiming 3,000-4,000 enemy soldiers as prisoners including two general officers and 30 pieces of artillery as special prizes. He went on to claim "The enemy are obstinate and seems to have found the last ditch. We have lost no organization, not even that of a company, while we have destroyed and captured one division (Johnson's), one brigade (Dole's), and one regiment entire of the enemy."

The battle which began at 0430 continued with diminishing volume as the shadow of evening cloaked the field. Still, shots were being fired even after midnight. Soldiers who fell in the darkness had the even greater misfortune of ending up on the missing lists and in unmarked graves. The grim spectacle, by the time it finally ended, had gone on for nearly 24 hours, a full day of fighting. Dawn would let both sides know the full consequences of their deadly labor.

Gouverneur Warren

The controversial Civil War general Gouverneur Warren was born in Cold Spring, New York, and graduated from West Point in 1850, later serving in the Engineers and as an instructor of Mathematics at the Military Academy. During the Civil War he would attain the heights of hero status, but by its end found his military career completely shattered.

Early in the war, Warren took the post of lieutenant colonel of the *5th New York* in which capacity he witnessed the Federal disaster at Big Bethel on 10 June 1861. A year later he was leading a brigade in McClellan's Peninsula Campaign. He served in combat command throughout 1862, seeing action on the fields of Second Bull Run, Antietam and Fredericksburg and rose to the rank of brigadier general. In the spring of 1863, he took a staff position as chief engineer for the *Army of the Potomac*. Warren would attain fame in this capacity during the battle of Gettysburg on 2 July 1863 when he noticed the significance of Little Round Top and put together a defense to hold it against a fierce Confederate attack. His actions saved the Union left from being broken, thus saving the Army of the Potomac from defeat.

After Gettysburg, Warren held the rank of major general and temporarily took command of the *II Corps* from the injured Winfield Scott Hancock during the Mine Run campaign of November-December 1863. Throughout Grant's 1864 offensive, Warren led the *V Corps* of the *Army of the Potomac*, but not with the distinction that might have been expected of him. Unfortunately, Warren failed to impress his superiors and, while competent, became known as overly cautious, with a penchant for seeing danger at every turn, and a font of unwanted advice.

The battle of Five Forks (1 April 1865) proved to be Warren's downfall. There Warren participated in a combined infantry and cavalry offensive against Confederate positions south of Petersburg under the hard fighting and acerbic Philip Sheridan. Both Sheridan and Grant had become increasingly dissatisfied with Warren's performance to the point of fearing that his inability to move quickly might endanger the operation. If Warren continued to be dilatory during the battle, Grant gave Sheridan permission to relieve the general of his command. Warren, ignorant that he was on probation, made two dire mistakes that sealed his fate: he arrived at the battlefield late and then accidentally almost marched away from the enemy he was supposed to attack. Sheridan replaced the unfortunate general with one of his division commanders, Charles Griffin, an event which tarnished Warren's reputation for years afterwards.

After the war, Warren labored to clear his name from the shame imposed upon him at Five Forks, finally winning a hearing 14 years after the fact. The court's conclusions exonerated the unhappy general, but this was too late to provide any satisfaction to Warren, the result being published months after his death on 8 August 1882.

CHAPTER IX

False Calm

13-16 May 1864

*H*eavy clouds hung over the rain and blood soaked ground of Spotsylvania at dawn on 13 May. In the Egyptian darkness of the new day, intermittently illuminated by the pale light of feeble camp fires, exhausted soldiers from both sides sought a desperately needed sleep on a field amongst the human carnage mixed with the broken accoutrements of war and amid plaintive calls for aid from wounded comrades. Too weary to care, some fatigued soldiers bunked with the dead as a member of the *141st Pennsylvania* recalled, "The dead were strewn so thickly that there was scarcely room for the living to lie down. The incessant rain had filled the ditches with water and transferred the soft fresh dirt into beds of mud. These beds were certainly *soft* enough to suit anybody, but were also decidedly moist. But when human nature is completely exhausted it is not particular where it finds rest. So our boys lay down in the ditches or on the muddy slopes, surrounded by the dying and the dead, and forgetful of the recent terrible strife and horrible surroundings, relapsed onto sound slumber." Unfortunately, a lengthy rest would, as of yet, be denied to Federal and Confederate soldiers as the events of 12 May had forced both armies to readjust their positions.

Lee's troops in the salient were the first on the move, retreating from the Mule Shoe in the early morning of 13 May. The first Confederate brigade to depart was Ramseur's battered command of North Carolinians which abandoned its position at 0300. An hour later Confederate brigade after brigade retreated from the ground they had bled so heavily to regain the day before. Their destination was the new entrenchments prepared at the base of the salient, on a slight crest paralleling the Brock Road. It was not long before their Yankee adversaries discovered this readjustment and reacted accordingly.

Just after dawn, the Union army undertook its ordered probe of the enemy position only to find the enemy had disappeared. *VI Corps* commander Wright reported at 0530 that the West Angle was empty of the enemy and his troops were occupying bloodied ground. In response to this report, Wright was ordered to continue advancing in a reconnaissance and his forces complied by moving down the west face of the salient. The *II Corps* also discovered the absence of the enemy and Hancock told his superiors his men had marched a half mile into the salient without facing any opposition. Like the *VI Corps*, the *II Corps* was ordered to keep moving forward and did so by pressing down the eastern face of the salient. Gouverneur Warren, meanwhile, was not as fortunate as his comrades. Enemy troops were still strongly positioned before his *V Corps,* making any forward movement by his command impossible.

Reports of the enemy's disappearance elated Grant who believed them to be indications of a general Confederate withdrawal. This prematurely optimistic assessment dissipated with the morning mists. By 0730, the advancing Federals were beginning to make fierce contact with their previously elusive enemy. Scattered skirmish fire began to intensify and grow fiercer as *II* and *VI Corps* troops began to close on the new Confederate position. The musketry brought down brigade commander Colonel Samuel Carrol of Gibbon's division with a wound, forcing him to leave command. By late morning the new Confederate line at the base of the salient was finally discovered by Federal forces, but no plans were made for an attack against

Union troops use the Confederates' entrenchments against them.

it that day. Instead of a more belligerent stance, the Federals merely retreated to the old Confederate works which were modified to face south against their old occupants. Lee and his troops were also disposed to let the enemy alone and enjoy a respite from combat.

The refusal to resume the fighting of 12 May was a wise decision for both sides as an accounting of the awful fighting the day before showed a terrible toll. Grant's army had been savaged with a huge loss of 7,000 Federal casualties. While most units maintained their integrity, others had suffered severely in terms of officers and men. The *5th Maine*, which had been at close quarters with the enemy near the Bloody Angle, lost the only captain that had been lucky enough to survive the fighting of 10 May. Another Maine regiment, the *32nd* in Potter's *IX Corps* division, emerged from the battle with a captain as its senior officer. Combining the Federal losses on 12 May with all the fighting from earlier in the month made Grant's stewardship of the *Army of the Potomac* appear disastrous. Dana reported back to Secretary of War Stanton that 36,872 men had been lost in nine days of active campaigning with almost a third of these missing, many of them being stragglers, shirkers or deserters. Such excessive casualties led one Federal to exclaim, "If we have to go in again, there won't be anybody left to keep the tally!" And the toll of battle was not the only source of the *Army of the Potomac*'s depletion. Many soldiers in three-year regiments had nearly completed terms of service and would soon be entitled to return home, depriving Grant of desperately needed combat veterans. The combined effect of battle losses and expiration of units' terms of service forced Hancock to consolidate Birney's and Mott's division into one under the command of the former, with the latter reverting to brigade command. This act finally ended the controversial role Mott's division played during the battle of Spotsylvania. The opinion of Mott's ability to lead and the value of his troops by the *II Corps'* leadership had never been high. Rightly or wrongly, the ineffectiveness of Mott's division would be blamed as a major reason for Federal failure to achieve victory at Spotsylvania on 12 May.

The Army of Northern Virginia did not suffer as severe a bloodletting as its adversary, but it had suffered a high toll indeed, one that its man-poor ranks could not well bear. Though

Junius Daniel

the exact number may never be known, nearly 6,000 Southern soldiers may have been lost in the 12 May fighting, with almost half being captured from Johnson's Division during Hancock's early morning attack. The huge number of captured Confederates was only exceeded in Lee's command by those so lost in Pickett's disastrous charge at Gettysburg on 3 July 1863. The units that had fought to regain the ground lost after the surprise of Johnson's Division and held the tip of the Mule Shoe had suffered as well in terms of dead and wounded. McGowan's Brigade lost nearly half its men during the period of its engagement, nearly 18 hours, a total of 86 killed, 248 wounded and 117 missing. Harris' command was in combat for two hours longer and also suffered half of its force as casualties. Of the Confederate commands, Johnson's Division of Walker's Brigade, Witcher's Brigade, Monaghan's Brigade, Steuart's Brigade and the once mighty Stonewall Brigade were only remnants of their former selves after the 12th. Lee consolidated the shattered units by consolidating the Virginians of the Stonewall Brigade, Witcher's Brigade and three regiments of Steuart's Brigade into one brigade. This, along with the Louisiana Brigade was assigned to Early's Division. Severe losses were especially felt in terms of officers killed, captured or wounded. The most notorious blow was the capture of division commander Major General Johnson and brigade commander Steuart. Brigadier General Abner Perrin had been killed in action and Daniel mortally wounded. The roll of officers wounded included James A. Walker, Samuel McGowan and S.D. Ramseur. Confederate leaders attempted to put a positive face on the heavy battle toll by claiming that the survivors had been steeled by the battle. Staff officer Taylor communicated this feeling when he wrote, "...sadly reduced though his [Lee's] army was, such was the metal of what remained that his lines, thus forcibly rectified, thereafter proved impregnable."

Battered as both armies were by the fighting of 12 May, the casualty figures alone can not tell the complete story of what happened that day. Other Civil War battles had been bloodier, had lasted longer and had yielded far more pivotal results, yet few could equal the horrific spectacles Spotsylvania's survivors painted of the battle's aftermath in their remembrances of the fight. A member of the *10th Vermont* remembered that the whole field, "was covered with a quivering mass of flesh." W.G. Tyler penned a description in more graphic detail, "Such a scene as we witnessed is beyond the power of pen to describe. The bodies of the fallen lay all over the field. Horses and men chopped into hash by the bullets, and appearing more like piles of jelly than the distinguishable forms of human life, were scattered all over the plain. Caissons and artillery carriages were cut into slivers.... The ground was soaked with blood and water, with here and there deeply dyed pools with the same ingredients." Gilbert Hays of the *63rd Pennsylvania* wrote, "The scene in our immediate front was one of the most fearful and repulsive that it was ever our fortune to behold. Words are inadequate to convey any idea of the sanguinary spectacle. Parties were engaged nearly all the day in burying the dead; but very few wounded were found, as those who had at first received only slight wounds, were unable to escape and were compelled to remain upon the field to be riddled again and again by the bullets of both friend and foe." Adjutant Muffley of the *148th Pennsylvania* allowed more emotion to escape into his recollections of the bloodbath, "I shrink from the attempt to describe the scene. It was a ghastly and horrible example of the organized brutality that we call war. No language can adequately portray the sickening spectacle. Imagine if you can, a line of entrenchment four hundred yards in length—a solid wall of timber and earth forming its front, with traverses extending at short intervals to the rear forming eight or ten pen-like enclosures half filled with dead and dying men. They lay in piles sometimes five men deep. Often the dead were lying upon the mortally wounded who groaned in their death agony and begged for water and prayed for death. Bodies hung upon the works in every form of mangling. Blood and mangling were everywhere and the sickening stench of the battlefield was over it all." The "saturnalia" of blood sometimes made scenes fantastically macabre as members of the *150th Pennsylvania* found near the West Angle, "...a caisson of a Sixth Corps battery, facing the fortifications, and perhaps not more than a hundred yards away, with its six horses still attached, but sunk to the earth, dead; the three drivers still in the saddle, likewise lifeless; while on the boxes rested six cannoneers, back to back, perforated with bullets, their inanimate bodies supporting one another almost in the attitude of duty. So natural was the position and appearance of these latter that the major could only convince himself that they were not alive only by reaching up and touching them."

Exceptionally awful were the trenches where both sides had fought so hard for so long. Brigadier General Lewis A. Grant, whose *Vermont Brigade* had seen some of the harshest fighting on the 12th wrote of the Angle, "The sight was terrible and sickening, much worse than at Bloody Lane (Antietam). There a great many dead men were lying in the road and across the rails of the torn down fences, and out in the cornfield; but they were not piled up several deep and their flesh was not so torn and mangled as at the angle." Lieutenant Colonel Henry Watkins of the *141st Pennsylvania* wrote of the battle that the "slaughter on both sides was beyond description." Of the West Angle he recorded, "Just at this point our own and the rebel dead lay in heaps, pierced, some of them, with hundreds of balls. So horrid and sickening a sight I never saw before." Gallway of the *95th Pennsylvania* wrote of the scene in the rifle pits, "Hundreds of Confederate dead or dying, lay piled over one another in those pits. The fallen lay three or four feet deep in some places, and, with but a few exceptions, they were shot in and about the head. Arms, accoutrements, ammunition, cannon, shot, and shell, and broken foliage were strewn about.... It was the most horrible sight I had ever witnessed." One soldier counted in a pit not over 50 feet in length 30 enemy dead with wounded mingled in or beneath them. Of the wounded some were to lie out in the field for days, exposed to the elements with open wounds and without food or water, before they were rescued. With Federals and Confederates in close quarters in some places, it was dangerous to hunt for and retrieve wounded comrades, forcing many parties to confine their searches at night. Many left on the field died from thirst, starvation, or neglect before their comrades could come to their aid.

The Union dead were treated with little ceremony, an unfortunate fact Bidwell of the *49th New York* was a witness of, "They were laid side by side in blankets. Enclosed in the blanket was the full name and rank of each one and at the head of each grave was placed a cracker box board with their names in large letters, so that their friends could easily identify them." Dead Confederates received fewer niceties from Yankee hands as a soldier from the *141st Pennsylvania* saw, "Many of the enemy's dead lay in the ditch which they had dug. They were left just as they fell, except that they were covered over with dirt shoveled from the top of the mounds they had thrown up. They had literally dug their own graves. Our own dead were buried in rear of our line, with no coffin or shroud; they were simply wrapped in their blankets, if they had any, and were buried wherever it was most convenient." Soldiers seeking comrades explored the mounds of mutilated flesh to find their fallen friends. At the Angle, bodies caught in the continuous fire had been so shot to pieces that they could only be moved in blankets. Major Nathan Church of the *26th Michigan* remarked of his efforts to find a friend on that

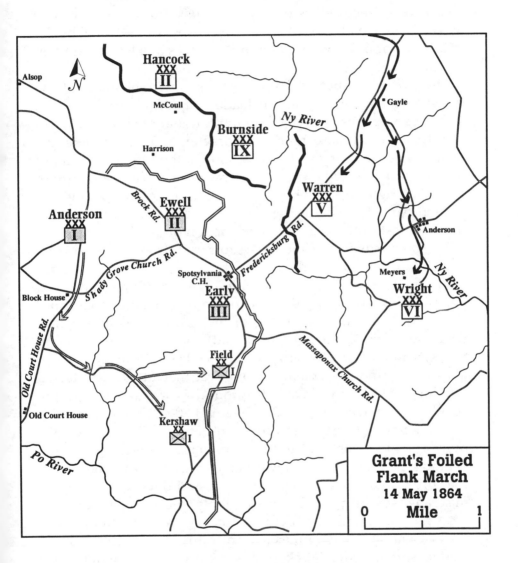

Alsop

Hancock
XXX
II

McCoull

Ny River

Gayle

Burnside
XXX
IX

Harrison

Warren
XXX
V

Anderson

Ewell
XXX
II

Anderson
XXX
I

Brock Rd.

Fredericksburg Rd.

Meyers

Wright
XXX
VI

Ny River

Shady Grove Church Rd.

Spotsylvania
C.H.

Early
XXX
III

Block House

Old Court House Rd.

Field
XX I

Old Court House

Massaponax Church Rd.

Kershaw
XX I

Po River

**Grant's Foiled
Flank March**
14 May 1864
Mile
0   1

field, "The dead were literally piled in heaps and it was a wonder how any one could have lived through those long hours of murderous conflict on which trees were cut down and the breast works themselves torn up by musket balls." One officer was only able to identify the mangled corpse of his friend by the reddish color of his whiskers and the pieces of a letter found on his mutilated person.

The ground at Spotsylvania was soaked with blood and flesh in a stalemated contest, but the leaders of both armies were still seeking an opening for victory. Grant, undaunted by his losses and true to his hardfighting character, looked to take the offensive. Concluding on the afternoon of the 13th that he might be able to find an advantage by getting on the Army of Northern Virginia's right, the general in chief laid out plans to slug that Confederate flank before it could be reinforced by elements from the rest of their line. Like the action on the 12th, the *Army of the Potomac* would make its assault with troops moved from one end of the army to the other. This time, the *V* and *VI Corps* would make the trek, a seven-mile night march around the *II* and *IX Corps*, to attack positions on and near the Fredericksburg Road. At 0400 on the morning of the 14th, the assault would begin with the *V* and *VI Corps* advancing in the direction Spotsylvania Court House with support from Burnside.

Grant's grand movement, a maneuver that, at its best, started off sluggishly and then slowly ground down to a frustrating snaillike pace, was supposed to begin at 2000. The first thing to go wrong was Warren's tardiness in getting his troops on the move, the *V Corps* only getting underway almost two hours behind schedule. The worst was yet to come. Once on the march, the corps floundered in the rain, mist and darkness through a miserable sea of mud. Understandably, the ranks became increasingly wearied and demoralized by their arduous task. Major General Warren himself went into the sad details of the trudge through the muck in his report on the action, "We marched all night through rain and mud, forded the Ny River once, and over routes none of us had travelled before. The night was intensely dark, and many of the men, from exhaustion and weariness, gave out; the line became disjointed and parts lost their way. The greatest pains were taken to mark the line by posting mounted men but it was impossible through the swamps and dense forest and pitchy darkness." A member of the *29th Massachusetts* agreed, "The mud was dreadful, the night dark, we forded streams up to our knees, and the mud all the time was over shoes." Major Nathaniel Michier of the *Corps of Engineers* recorded, "The wretched condition of the roads and the terrible darkness of night, added to the great fatigue of the troops, made it almost impossible to affect the change." Soldiers suffering through these conditions could not realistically be expected to carry on a major attack with much success.

The mud march played havoc with Grant's plans. At the appointed hour for the attack, only 1,200 exhausted soldiers of Griffin's division were in position on the Fredericksburg Road to attack. Three-and-a-half hours later only 1,300 more of Griffin's men and 1,300 of Cutler's could be counted on to assail the enemy. Wright's *VI Corps* had also had little luck in speedily reaching its destination. The force was on the march around 0300 and only in the vicinity of Warren's position on the Fredericksburg Road after 0900. The attempted attack had become an embarrassing fiasco and was wisely called off.

Though the bad weather had called off a major confrontation on the 14th, a brief tussle occurred which tarnished Emory Upton's reputation and embarrassed Major General Meade. The ground contended for was a small elevation southeast of the Fredericksburg Road called Myers' Hill, significant in that it offered a good view of the Confederate position. The hill was originally occupied by a small Confederate force that was easily swept away when Warren decided he wanted the position. Upton's brigade of less than 800 men was later called upon to hold it; however, the usually pugnacious Upton was concerned he could not maintain his position there before a strong enemy counterattack and called for reinforcements. Two New Jersey regiments arrived to help, but even these weren't enough to stop an afternoon Confederate counterattack of two brigades which emerged from woods in front of his troops. The Yankees were

*Robert O. Tyler led an
infantry division of con-
verted heavy artillery-
men at Spotsylvania.*

swept from the hill and along with them fled a flustered General Meade who was visiting the area and very nearly got captured when the enemy attacked. An indignant Meade ordered an attack to retake the hill, a move that proved unnecessary since the Confederates decided to leave before the Federal attack got underway.

The events at Myers' Hill had a far greater impact than an isolated skirmish action. Both Wright and Warren were concerned that the fight there meant their new position on the Federal left might be in danger of being flanked. This concern led Meade to request that the *II Corps* march to defend the left from enemy aggression, a request Grant agreed to, but with the provision that one division be left behind to protect Burnside's right flank. Birney's division was detailed to remain behind while the two other *II Corps* divisions made their march at 0400 to the Federal left through mud ankle and even knee deep in some places.

Meanwhile the Confederate leadership was surveying their

enemy's movements and reacting to them. Lee's troops discovered Warren's departure early on the 14th when troops entered the *V Corps* lines to find them deserted. At 1230, Early reported the enemy was moving to the Army of Northern Virginia's right, an observation confirmed less than three hours later when cavalry commander Rooney Lee reported the new positions of the *V* and *VI Corps* on the Confederate left. The Southern commander responded by shifting Field's Division of the First Corps from the left to the right to the south of Spotsylvania and later sent the rest of the corps to counter the enemy threat on the Confederate right.

For their own part, the Federals stayed in their positions without attacking for the next three days after their 14 May moves and dug in. Troops of the *V* and *VI Corps* worked to extend their trenches southward establishing positions for batteries as well as examining the country for routes southward. Meanwhile thousands of reinforcements joined the Federal army, more than replenishing the losses of 12 May. The first to come were 1,500 troops of Colonel Warner's regiment which were ordered to join Grant's *Vermont Brigade* on 15 May. The next day a 1,600 man brigade of four rookie New York regiments arrived called the *Irish Legion*. Its effectiveness was considered dubious since many of its members were reported to have arrived inebriated. On the 18th came the *Corcoran Legion* which joined Gibbon's division. The most important arrival was a division of *Heavy Artillery* units under Brigadier General R.O. Tyler. The troops of this force had been culled from units that had spent most of the war in a leisurely defense of Washington, D.C., occupying fortifications that had yet to come under a serious threat. These troops were more veterans of fancy dress parades before important officials than of battlefield combat. Their relaxed lifestyle was doomed the moment Grant ordered many of the *Heavy Artillery* regiments into the field for regular duty as infantry, much to the delight of veterans of combat. When "heavies" marched into the *Army of the Potomac*'s camp at Spotsylvania with clean uniforms and polished muskets, their weather and battle worn comrades cheerfully called out, "How

Union heavy artillery units prepare to move out as infantry, their straight lines and smart appearance the result of several years' "dress parade" soldiering in Washington.

are you, heavies? Is this work heavy enough for you?" Together Tyler's division and the *Corcoran Legion* numbered 8,000 men.

Along with the reinforcements came heartening news of victories being won on fields elsewhere as Federal forces seemed to be prevailing on every major front. Ben Butler reported on 15 May the capture of the outer works at Drewry's Bluff on the James River near Richmond and that his cavalry had cut the railroad and telegraph lines south of that city. The hard riding Phil Sheridan was out wreaking havoc by tearing up the Virginia Central Railroad, but had pinned a more important feather in his cap, the death of Jeb Stuart, who had fallen with a mortal wound during a cavalry battle at Yellow Tavern on 11 May. In West Virginia, William Averell reported the destruction of a Confederate supply depot and the destruction of the New River Bridge on the Virginia and Tennessee Railroad line. In Georgia, Billy Sherman's forces had driven Johnston's Army of Tennessee out of Dalton and were proceeding south onto the heart of the Confederacy.

While both armies squared off occasional skirmishes broke out and soldiers attended to other matters. Tom Rosser's cavalry on 15 May wandered into the rear of the Union army on a reconnaissance mission where his troops raided some hospitals and rounded up prisoners. During the brief flurry of activity some of the Confederate troopers tangled with the *23rd U.S. Colored Troops*. Other soldiers engaged in more passive pursuits. On the same day as Rosser's action, a group of Confederates found a nest of four baby bunnies that had been abandoned by their mother. The animals might have provided a feast for ravenous soldiers, but these veterans adopted the animals and built a shelter to protect the animals from the elements. One of the regiment wrote, "I do not know that I ever saw men more solicitous for the welfare of anything than were those grizzly warriors for those bunnies." Despite this respite for some Confederates, Lee had the rest of Anderson's Corps, Kershaw's Division, march to join Field's Division on the army's right. The soldiers started their march during the last moments of the 15th, arriving at their intended distination a few hours later.

On 16 May, Lee found time to write a letter to his wife, a note that expressed his feelings at the moment of one of his greatest trials, "As I write I am expecting the sound of our guns any moment. I grieve over the loss of our gallant officers and men, and miss their aid and sympathy. A more zealous, ardent, brave and devoted soldier than Stuart the Confederacy cannot have. Praise be God for having sustained us so far."

And while a relative calm had descended, both sides were to endeavor to defeat the other one more time, briefly bringing back the sounds of fierce musketry and cannonading to the fields, farms, and trenches near Spotsylvania.

Heavy Artillery

The battles around Spotsylvania contained many odd, famous, and infamous events, one being the *Heavy Artillery*'s first major engagements outside of the trenches around Washington. Though these troops had seen little combat before their participation in Grant's campaign, their actions at Spotsylvania and on later fields of battles marked them as some of the best Union fighting units of the war.

The close proximity of Washington D.C. to the Southern Confederacy meant the National capital could easily come under the threat of an enemy attack or isolation. To protect the city, miles upon miles of trenches were constructed and within them were hundreds of huge heavy guns and dozens of mortars. The *Heavy Artillery* regiments, or *Heavies* as they were called, helped operate these defenses, being trained both as infantry and cannoneers. Since Washington had never come under a significant attack before 1864, the troops assigned to protect it had a leisurely life of pomp and drill with whatever comforts they could afford. These sometimes included fixed barracks with beds, ample quantities of supplies and food, comfortable hospitals and sometimes even a regimental library. The absence of combat also meant the ranks of *Heavy Artillery* units remained rather large. Because they rarely engaged in battle, they rarely took casualties, a fact that encouraged enlistments into their ranks since their volunteers could abstain from risking their lives while having the distinction of serving in uniform. By the battle of Spotsylvania, a regiment of *Heavy Artillery* numbered about 1,800 men, almost the size of a brigade or division that was serving in the field.

Grant, believing the *Army of the Potomac* to be the principle guardian of Washington even while on the offensive, changed the lives of the *Heavy Artillery* units forever. To the delight of the soldiers of the *Army of the Potomac*, he reduced them in effect to regular infantry troops, ordering them to leave the blissful security of their entrenchments and join his march south for Richmond. Two regiments, the *6th* and *15th New York Heavy Artillery* joined the *Army of the Potomac* while it was in the Wilderness. These were organized into a brigade under Colonel J. Howard Kitching and assigned to serve as an infantry force with the *Artillery Reserve*, though they were later detached to serve with other elements of the army. Next to arrive was the *1st Vermont Heavy Artillery*, 1,500 men in all, which entered the ranks of the *VI Corps' Vermont Brigade* on 14 May. Five more regiments, the *1st Maine Heavy Artillery*, the *1st Massachusetts Heavy Artillery*, the *2nd*, *7th* and *8th New York Heavy Artillery* were organized into a division under Brigadier General Robert O. Tyler which joined the *II Corps* on 18 and 19 May 1864.

While their lack of combat experience might have led some to believe that these units would panic on the field of battle or be entirely useless, their first exposure to combat at Spotsylvania proved otherwise. The *Heavy Artillery* including the *1st Maine Heavy Artillery*, the *1st Massachusetts Heavy Artillery*, the *1st, 2nd* and *4th New York Heavy Artillery*, saw some fierce combat against Confederate veterans of Ewell's Second Army Corps on 19 May 1864. The *Heavies'* fight on open ground earned them the admiration of friend and foe alike, but cost them severely in casualties, some 1,500 men.

In subsequent engagements, the *Heavies* would engage in terrible fighting, again exhibiting daring bravado, but with terrible consequences. Near Petersburg on 18 June, the *1st Maine Heavy Artillery* advanced unsupported against a strong Confederate position. The enemy fire nearly decimated the attacking force, killing and wounding nearly 600 of the 900-man regiment. The loss was the greatest sustained by any Northern regiment in battle.

The *Heavy Artillery* served out the rest of the war as regular infantry units, adopting the worn soldier look and experience while leaving the halcyon days of their Washington service to distant memory. However, as the battle record of the *Heavies* made clear, they were one of the more reliable reinforcements the *Army of the Potomac* received in Grant's campaign against Richmond.

Fights Mit Sigel
Franz Sigel's Shenandoah Campaign

An important part of Grant's master plan of waging war on all fronts was to finally deny the Shenandoah Valley to Confederate use. This fertile region had been a breadbasket for the South, providing Confederate armies with a bounty of supplies. Confederate forces had also used the Valley as a highway for their military operations, including the invasion of the North in 1863. Throughout the war, Union commanders had attempted to seize this area through force of arms only to suffer defeat after humiliating defeat. It was in the Shenandoah Valley that the legendary Stonewall Jackson won some of his most fantastic victories of the war at First Winchester (25 May 1862), Cross Keys (8 June 1862), and Port Republic (9 June 1862). In the spring of 1864, another campaign was to be launched in conjunction with other Union offensives in the East and West.

The mission seemed doomed from the start. The commander chosen for the operation in the Shenandoah was Major General Franz Sigel. Sigel's career throughout the war thus far was lackluster to say the least. Attaining high command primarily through his political prowess and his ability to attract German Americans to shoulder muskets in Union armies, he had proven an embarrassment on the battlefield. Worse still, the army he was to command, 9,800 men in all, contained a sizable number of troops of questionable fighting quality. Many of these had done little military service besides garrison duty. Two regiments of Ohio infantry that had seen active service had been captured in the summer of 1863 and were later exchanged. These were considered completely useless. Directing these commands was Sigel's staff, many of whom were German themselves and had a limited command of the English language. A grim harbinger of the fate of Sigel's offensive occurred during his army's grand review on 28 April, which dissolved into mass confusion.

On 29 April, the Federal advance began with Sigel's force leaving Martinsurg, West Virginia. Sigel slowly moved south, reaching Winchester, Virginia, on 1 May where he stopped for a drill for his troops, an engagement which proved to be a fiasco. One regiment charged right out of the exercise and was not recalled. Another unit on picket duty was completely forgotten about until the drill was over. Instead of improving the fighting prowess of the troops, it only cemented their low morale and distrust for their commanders whom they labeled as foreign adventurers and fools.

On 10 May, while the *Army of the Potomac* battled the Army of Northern Virginia, Sigel's army continued its march through the Valley with its eventual object being the crossroads town of New Market. Increasingly, Sigel's troops came into contact with Confederate cavalry and word had been received of a large Southern force active in the area. Still, Sigel decided to split his army up at Woodstock, Virginia, by advancing 2,350 men under Colonel August Moor on 14 May to make a reconnaissance toward New Market while the rest of his force remained behind. Moor pressed his troops ahead aggressively through a fierce rainstorm and resistance from Confederate cavalry, but, despite his best efforts, he could not reach New Market before nightfall and camped north of the town. Meanwhile, a Confederate infantry force was marching in Moor's direction from the south. Its mission, to whip Sigel and save the Shenandoah Valley for the Confederacy.

Sigel did not have to worry about facing superior troop strengths, but he did have to face superior generalship. Scraping together a force to meet him was former politician John C. Breckinridge, a two-term U.S. Representative from Kentucky and vice-president during the Buchanan administration. Breckinridge had proved himself in the Western Theater on battlefields like Chickamauga and Missionary Ridge. Brought east to command the Department of Southwestern Virginia, he would find that his first major task was thwarting Sigel. Breckinridge scoured his already man-poor department for whatever troops he could find to contend with the Union threat. Eventually, he mustered some 5,000 troops including militia units and a force of 258 teenage cadets from the Virginia Military Institute (VMI). Breckinridge, headquartered at Dublin, Virginia, began moving north on 5 May. Nine days later, he was south of New Market and ready for a fight. News of Moor's engagement with Confederate cavalry spurred Breckinridge to get his forces to the town for a confrontation.

On the morning of 15 May, Breckinridge's infantry joined with his cavalry north of New Market. The political general decided to gamble boldly and attack the enemy rather than allow him the opportunity to mass his larger forces. Around 1000, the Confederates began to advance, charging into the Federal position now commanded by Major General Julius Stahel-Szamwald. At first, Breckenridge's brave play seemed enough to win the day. The flustered General Stahel thought he was outnumbered by the attackers and ordered a retreat to a stronger position in the rear. However, the Federals still had greater numbers and the men still marching toward the scene of battle could enable them to retrieve their fortunes, if they arrived in time.

Sigel himself arrived around noon to take command amd supervise the creation of a new Union defensive line on elevated ground. Breckinridge tried to keep the offensive going, charging his troops against the new enemy position only to have them suffer terribly under destructive blasts of canister from Federal batteries. Though he was loathe to commit his VMI cadets, Breckinridge sent them into the action to bolster his faltering attack. In a strange twist during the fog of battle, Breckinridge was saved by Sigel's fumbling attempts to launch an attack of his own. The first try was a charge by 2,000 cavalryman under General Stahel launched at 1445. Instead of scattering the enemy, the Yankee troopers only rode into a pocket of fire where they were quickly mangled and sent fleeing. Sigel then ordered his infantry to move forward only to have them suffer the same ignominious fate as the cavalry. Heartened, Breckinridge's forces continued their own advance, breaking and brushing away the remnants of Sigel's force and sending them retreating north. The VMI cadets seized a battle trophy of their own during the final charge when they advanced 50 yards in the mud to capture a Yankee cannon which they turned on its former owners.

Sigel finally gave up the contest, ordering a retreat north to Cedar Creek where he would reform his battered army. His part in Grant's offensives on all fronts was over as Halleck wrote Grant, "He will do nothing, but run. He never did anything else." Some 830 men were lost in Sigel's fiasco which inevitably ruined what was left of his reputation and led to his removal from command.

As New Market ruined Sigel, it raised Breckinridge. The battle was both an important laurel for him and for the Confederacy as he had saved the Shenandoah Valley from Northern invasion, allowing it to remain in Southern hands for months to come. More importantly, with Sigel's threat nullified, Breckinridge's troops could now march to reinforce General Lee's Army of Northern Virginia and make good much of the losses that army had suffered in the battles against Grant and the *Army of the Potomac* during May. Sigel's role in Grant's grand plan for the summer thus had the opposite effect that had been intended.

As for the VMI Cadets, 57 of their numbers were among the 580 casualties Breckinridge's force had suffered during the battle, 10 had been killed and 47 wounded. Their sacrifices had helped seal the victory and win them a lasting honor which is still celebrated at the military academy to this day.

CHAPTER X

Return to Hell's Half Acre

17-18 May 1864

*U*ndaunted by his failure to attack the Army of Northern Virginia's right, Grant considered the possibility of an attack elsewhere. Grant's command was aware that the Confederates had reacted to the movement of Warren and Wright to the Federal left, and the corresponding Confederate counter-manuever of shifting their forces to the right might have made their left flank weaker. In particular, chief of staff Humphreys and corps commander Wright saw this attractive opportunity for an assault of some kind and envisioned an attack with only the *VI Corps*. Grant, heartened by a day of good weather, agreed while building upon the plan, ordering an assault with both the *II Corps* and *VI Corps* at 0400 on 18 May. The target was the new enemy entrenchments at the base of the Mule Shoe. This meant the Federals would have to advance from and over the very ground which had been fought over during the conflagration of combat on 12 May, now known, for obvious reasons, as "Hell's Half-Acre."

Grant's plan, of course, required more marching by Federal troops, even the retracing of much of the movements made over the past week. At 1900 on 17 May, Meade ordered Hancock to move his troops by night to the vicinity of the Landrum House

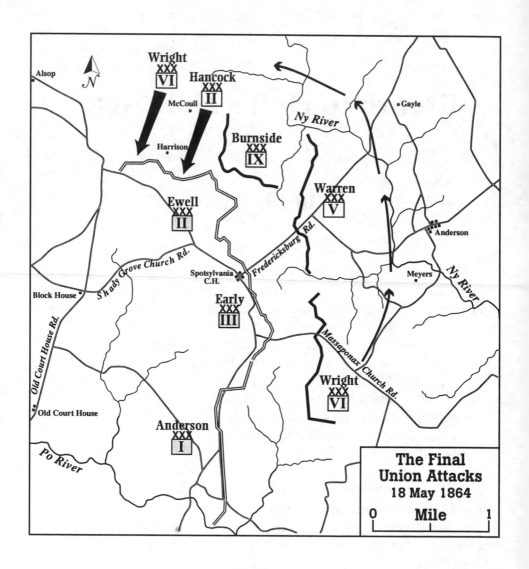

The Final
Union Attacks
18 May 1864

0   Mile   1

where his charge against the Confederate position would be launched. Wright's *VI Corps* was to march from its current position around the entire Union army to the *II Corps* right where it would jump off for its attack. Unlike the mud march of four days earlier, good weather prevailed, enabling the Yankees to reorder their lines for the day's hard work with relative ease. By 0300, Hancock reported that he had Barlow's and Gibbon's divisions preparing for their drive in the Landrum fields and the *VI Corps* was taking position on his right. But not all went as planned. The *VI Corps* experienced difficulty getting into attack position while Tyler's rookie division of the *II Corps* was tardy. Frustrating as these delays were, Hancock's troops went forward at 0430 with Barlow's and Gibbon's divisions, both arrayed in two lines, while the rest of the corps remained in reserve. The only force on hand for assistance from the *VI Corps* was Neill's division.

By the time the Yankee lines surged forward, the Confederates had prepared an unpleasant reception. Contrary to the guesses of Federal commanders that the enemy left had been weakened, there was ample force there to fend off the assault. Rodes' and Gordon's Divisions of Ewell's corps were on hand, well entrenched on a low rise behind a huge network of abatis in front and supported by 24 guns. The ground before them provided ample opportunities to sweep any attacking force with canister and musketry. Even worse for the Federals was the ground over which they would have to advance, littered with the carnage of previous fighting made worse by exposure to the rain and sun. Blackened corpses were strewn about everywhere, some partially concealed in shallow graves with a leg or arm sticking out while others, who had been shot while climbing through abatis, hung on the cut branches and looked from afar like they were standing. The stench from the rotting flesh was awful as Union Major W.G. Mitchell recounted, "...as a portion of the dead... had been buried, the stench which arose from them, was so sickening and terrible that many of the men and officers became deathly sick from it. The appearance of the dead who had been exposed to the sun so long was horrible in the extreme as we marched past and over them—a sight never to be forgotten by those who witnessed it."

Barlow's men advanced over the ground of the East Angle, where the second line halted while the first advanced into the woods on the interior of the Mule Shoe. Before the Confederate position they found a huge network of abatis nearly 100 feet in length, almost impossible to cut through. Taking heavy fire from musketry and cannon fire, Barlow had his troops lie down for cover. Gibbon's division also left its second line behind at the old entrenchments while the first pressed forward through the Mule Shoe, entering the McCoull fields to encounter heavy fire, advancing only as far as the old Confederate reserve entrenchments before it ground to a halt. Gibbon's second line pushed forward and with some its troops advancing closer to the enemy position, managed to reach the abatis in front of the enemy line, but got no further. Neill's brigades advanced down the western face of the salient with its left in the McCoull field. The *VI Corps* division only got as far as the old reserve works before the punishing enemy fire brought it to a halt. Roe of the *10th Massachusetts* noted of the advance, "...they saluted our approach with spherical case, canister and rifle balls, in no stinted measure. If a man exposed himself at all, his name was quickly added to the list of casualties." On the right of Roe's regiment was a captain of the *7th Maine* who could see the Rebels reloading their cannon and just before they would fire he would yell out to his comrades, "Look out boys, here it comes." Burnside also contributed to the attack with groups of Potter's and Crittenden's lines advancing through a fog toward the enemy line facing their line, but were repulsed by enemy fire. Informed of the failure of the Federal attacks and the small likelihood of any success, Meade brought a halt to the operation. The *II Corps* withdrew, while the *VI Corps* returned to its position on the *V Corps* right.

The abysmal failure of his attack on the Confederate lines was not the only disappointment Grant had to face on 18 May. Word had come from the Shenandoah that Franz Sigel had been defeated at the battle of New Market and was fleeing north.

Butler's advance had likewise been repulsed from the gates of Richmond by a numerically inferior army under Confederate P.G.T. Beauregard. Worse still, Butler was now blockaded in the peninsula of Bermuda Hundred, locked safely away where he could pose no further threat to the Confederate capital or anything else. Farther away in Louisiana, an offensive up the Red River by Union Major General Nathaniel Banks had been defeated and his troops were wandering back to safety. Grant was disappointed by all these failures across the board as he later recorded in his memoirs, "All this news was very discouraging. All of it must have been known by the enemy before it was by me, in fact, the good news (for the enemy) must have been known to him at the moment I thought he was in despair, and his anguish had already been relieved when we were enjoying his supposed discomfiture. But this was no time for repining." Indeed, Grant would remain true to the promise he sent President Lincoln nearly two weeks earlier, "Whatever happens, there will be no turning back."

However, Grant would not be keeping his earlier promise, "to fight it out on this line if it takes all summer." Satisfied that the opportunity to defeat Lee could not be had at Spotsylvania, he wanted to move the fighting on to a more fruitful battlefield somewhere closer to Richmond by baiting a hook with the entire *II Corps*. His plan required that Hancock march his corps south via the Fredericksburg Railroad as far south as it could go, getting in between Lee and Richmond. A Union corps detached from the main *Army of the Potomac* might be too tempting a target for Lee to pass up, forcing him to give up his formidable fortifications around Spotsylvania while going off in a pursuit. Grant would then race to link up with Hancock once again for the battle which might take place on more open ground. If Lee didn't bite, Hancock's advance could serve as the beginning of a regular turning movement, and the rest of the army would march to link up with the *II Corps* anyway and get between Lee and Richmond. Pursuant to this plan, Grant sent 100 artillery pieces back to Washington, DC so his marches would not be slowed by large artillery trains. He also informed Halleck of his intention to change his supply base from Fredericksburg to Port Royal so he could draw sustenance for his army up the Rappahannock River.

On 18 May, the *Army of the Potomac* began to march yet again, with commands once again negotiating the ground they had crossed and recrossed throughout the confrontation at Spotsylvania. First to move was Tyler's *Heavy Artillery* division marching to the Federal left around the vicinity of the Anderson House southeast of the Fredericksburg Road. The *VI Corps* followed Tyler, reaching the Anderson House before mid-day. By late afternoon, Wright's divisions set up defensive positions east of Spotsylvania and south of the Fredericksburg Road from Myers' Farm to Anderson's Mill. The next day, they would close up on the Confederate right flank facing them. Hancock joined Wright on the night of 18 May, making for the Federal left and going into camp at Anderson's Mill. Burnside's *IX Corps* marched early in the morning of 19 May, reaching the Myer house at 0545 only to find its path blocked by Wright's men on their way to follow orders to close up on the Confederate position. Burnside had his troops march south to form up on the *VI Corps* left all the way to the Massaponax Church Road.

Grant's baited line was ready to be cast. Hancock received orders at 1330 on 19 May to move out at 0200 the next day, marching 20 miles to Milford Station via Bowling Green, attempting to get south of the Mattapony River if possible. The soldiers in the ranks were glad to finally have the chance to get away from the fetid killing ground of Spotsylvania. Lieutenant Colonel Watkins wrote of his displeasure in remaining there in a 18 May letter, "I have eaten supper from an old oil cloth spread over the buried remains of brave soldiers, amid the most noisome smell one can imagine. I hope we will move from this spot soon. The stench is intolerable and the associations by no means pleasing." Indeed, the army would be moving, but not before one last battle was fought.

With the Federals maneuvering for their advance south, the battlefield initiative now fell into Confederate hands, the first such opportunity for Lee to strike back during the campaign at

Spotsylvania. Grant's most recent reshuffling of his position gave Lee an opening he had been looking for; he knew the Federals had pulled forces away from their right to operate on their left, perhaps their right flank had been weakened to the point it might be vulnerable to a counterattack. To find out, Lee ordered Ewell's corps to locate the right of the *Army of the Potomac* and possibly get around it, thereby cutting the Federals off from their supplies.

Ewell's force, numbering about 6,000 men after recent fighting, would first march as far northwest as needed to get past the enemy flank and then veer northeast in the direction of Fredericksburg, hopefully into the rear of the enemy's army. The advance began between 1400-1500 on 19 May with the infantry of Rodes' and Gordon's divisions and Wade Hampton with Rosser's cavalry leaving the safety of the Confederate entrenchments. Their first route was up the Brock Road toward Alsop's where they would take a right and move northeast along the Gordon Road toward the Armstrong House. Not long after the troops got underway, there were indications that the movement was not going to go smoothly. The roads the army was using were poor and this forced some of the corps' artillery back. When Ewell's column got to the Ny, the river was found to be so swollen from recent rains that the rest of the artillery was not able to get across. The corps commander was not deterred, he would march on without his heavy guns, a decision that worried Lee, causing him to have Early extend his line in the attempt to offer some cover to the column on the move. When Ewell's forces reached the Armstrong House, the cavalry continued on to the northeast, while the infantry turned southeast. Ewell's divisions reached the Stevens House where they went into line, Rodes pausing to allow Gordon to go east and set up on his left. As the Confederates continued their advance southeast, their lead brigade, Ramseur's North Carolinians of Rodes' Division, began to encounter rifle firing from Federals of the *4th New York Heavy Artillery* around 1630-1700. Ramseur drove them back and pressed on.

The Confederate attack was falling on the rookie troops of

Tyler's and Kitching's oversized brigades of *Heavy Artillery* troops, Grant's most recent reinforcements. These raw troops were about to see their first battle against some of Lee's fiercest veterans. Kitching's division had spotted Confederate activity and Tyler had moved northwest up the Fredericksburg road to head it off. After the *4th New York Heavy Artillery* got involved in firing on the Harris Farm, Tyler's division moved in that direction. The *1st Massachusetts Heavy Artillery* was the next Federal unit infantry to arrive at the Harris Farm once the battle began, probing the enemy position with a battalion which suffered a severe repulse, leaving its commander severely wounded and many of its troops departing the field. Ramseur's Brigade, pressing its advantage, tried to advance several times against the Federals, now coming on the *4th New York Heavy Artillery* near the Alsop Farm, northeast of Harris'. Ramseur's brigade encountered a tough fire, including flanking rifle fire from Massachusetts troops still on the field and canister from two Federal guns. First brought to a halt and then forced to retreat a couple hundred yards, Ramseur was joined by Grimes' and Ramseur's brigades of Rodes' Division.

The Federal side was receiving reinforcements as well in the form of the *1st Maine Heavy Artillery* and the *2nd New York Heavy Artillery*, which had fought off some enemy troops threatening a supply train on the Fredericksburg Road, and now extended the line opposing Ewell to the northeast. Also joining these Heavies was the *8th New York Heavy Artillery*, and the *1st Maryland* infantry which had just arrived at the front from a restful Veteran furlough. These new Federal arrivals were able to get on the flank of Gordon's division on the left of Rodes', setting at first that division, followed by Rodes', into a brief retreat.

As the raging battle devolved into a stalemate, both sides fed reinforcements to the area of confrontation to help decide the issue. The intense firing caused Meade to order Hancock at 1730 to send a division at all possible haste to help, and follow with his entire corps. Birney's division was the closest force Hancock had available and that was dispatched on the double quick.

Warren was also asked to help and he responded by sending the *Maryland Brigade* and the *Pennsylvania Reserve Division*. Artillery was dispatched to the scene of the action as well.

Lee was also concerned by the battle, especially with Ewell's Corps being engaged far away from the rest of his army and the safety of the Confederate entrenchments. To help matters, he had Early advance against Warren to draw Federal attention elsewhere, an attack that only managed to drive in some enemy pickets, but do little else.

Meanwhile the heavy fighting continued with the Heavies standing up in lines with almost veteran precision, firing away at the enemy position. Staff officer Horace Porter, sent to survey the action by Grant, reported to General Tyler. Porter tried to give an optimistic view on the battle, telling the division commander, "Tyler, you are in luck today. It isn't everyone who has a chance to make such a debut on joining the army." Tyler replied, "As you see, my men are raw hands at this sort of work, but they are behaving like veterans." Reinforced by more Heavies and *II Corps* troops, the Federals tried to advance against the Confederate position, only to find they could make no headway. Ewell, by that point, realized that the best he could do was hold on where he was, retreating under cover of darkness when night came. He himself was in the thick of the fighting, having his horse shot under him and falling painfully to the ground. Fortunately, Hampton's command of cavalry rejoined Ewell, after causing some trouble in the Union rear as far as the Orange Plank Road, reinforcing the embattled ranks with troopers and cannons they had managed to bring along on the journey.

By 2100, the battle slowly came to a halt in the darkness Ewell had been waiting for. An hour later, his troops began to withdraw from the field. Around 900 Rebels had been lost in the fighting and all for no purpose, as Ewell's movement had failed to accomplish any grand objectives. Many of the Federals who fell in the battle were the rookie heavies who became the talk of both armies for their out-in-the-open stand and shoot fighting style. Their bravado had cost them dear, but it had also won

A dead Confederate from Ewell's command, possibly dragged into a more dramatic position by an enterprising Northern photographer.

these fighters, who had previously been derided as "bandbox" soldiers, well deserved respect. One of Hancock's soldiers who saw the Heavies in action wrote, "The ground was literally covered with dead and wounded of the heavy artillery regiments. Not having previous experience in campaigning and actual fighting, the officers and men of these regiments neglected the precautions which veterans take, and instead of lying down and availing themselves of natural protections, had chosen their position on the crest of a hillock, where they stood erect, as on dress parade on battalion drill, thus furnishing admirable targets for the Confederates who fought, as usual behind trees and boulders." One Confederate veteran of the

Harris field later told his captors in the *39th Massachusetts*. "I saw your men march on this field, not deployed, but like soldiers on parade, take aim and fire a volley straight from the shoulder. You seemed to me the biggest men I ever seen. You were so near that I noticed all wore clean shirts. There was the most perfect discipline and indifference to danger I ever saw. It was the talk of our men." The cost of such daring was heavy, over 1,500 casualties in all, as a group of staff officers found out while riding in the vicinity of the field that night after the fighting. They came upon a row of men near the Fredericksburg Road, all stretched out in apparent peaceful slumber. One officer tried to wake one of the soldiers by shaking him and shouting, "Get up! What do you mean by going to sleep at such a time as this?" When the soldier did not stir, it became apparent that he and his comrades were not asleep at all, they had been shot down in battle and lay in ranks where they fell.

Richard Ewell

Richard Ewell (1817-1872) was born outside of Washington before his family moved to Prince William County, Virginia. He graduated from West Point in 1840 to serve in the dragoons. Up to 1861 Ewell's service record included combat in Indian campaigns and the Mexican War in which he won a brevet rank of captain. He left the army on 7 May 1861 to join Southern ranks as a colonel.

Originally a cavalry officer, Ewell soon became a brigadier general of an infantry brigade which he commanded at First Bull Run. He later served with Stonewall Jackson during his famous Shenandoah Valley campaign. Ewell initially felt Jackson was insane, but soon came to appreciate his commander's military abilities. Wounded seriously at Groveton on 28 August 1862, Ewell lost a leg, but won a wife, falling in love with the nurse who attended him. Ewell later returned in May of 1863 to command on the battlefield though he had to be lifted up on and strapped into his saddle to ride a horse.

Ewell took command of Stonewall Jackson's corps after his old commander's death. He was first tried as a corps commander in one of the most important episodes of the war, the Gettysburg Campaign. He did not perform well, ordering some ineffective assaults on Culp's Hill on 2 and 3 July 1863 that were of little consequence to the great events going on elsewhere. During the Wilderness and Spotsylvania campaigns the next year, Ewell proved more able, fending off massed infantry charges. A fall from his horse at Spotsylvania gave him an injury that limited his ability to command. By the end of May his command was given to Jubal Early and unlimited leave was offered to the ailing general who refused it in order to remain with his men. Ewell desperately attempted to return to his old position, even appealing to President Jefferson Davis. His attempts were to no avail and he reluctantly accepted transfer to the Department of Richmond. He supervise the defenses of the Southern capital during the closing stage of the war and was captured at Sayler's Creek after the city's fall. After the war, he resided on his wife's farm in Tennessee until his death in 1872.

Ewell has been criticized as a decent division commander who found his ability for decisiveness and boldness lacking when commanding a corps. His troops maintained respect for him even though their nicknames for him seem a bit silly, "Old Bald Head" and "Baldy Dick."

Richard Anderson

Though perhaps not was well known as Stonewall Jackson or James Longstreet, South Carolinian Richard Anderson was one of Lee's most reliable corps commanders. Anderson himself was from a distinguished military heritage, being the son of a Revolutionary War hero. He sought a military career of his own by entering West Point, graduating in the class of 1842 with a lackluster record. Commisioned in the dragoons, he saw action against Native Americans and was commended for his service in the Mexican War.

South Carolina's secession after Lincoln's election made Anderson tender his services to his native state. He took command of the 1st South Carolina Infantry and was involved in his state's momentous attack on Fort Sumter. After the rest of the nation collapsed into the fury of Civil War, Anderson served under Braxton Bragg in Florida, but was transferred to a more active field of duty in Virginia where he commanded troops in Johnston's and later Lee's army. His meritorious service during the Peninsula Campaign and the Seven Days battles won distinction and notice from superiors.

Anderson was promoted to major general and given divisional command in which capacity he fought in most of the major battles in the East during the war. When Longstreet was wounded in the Wilderness on 6 May 1865, Anderson took his place, a decision that was popular with the men, who wept when he rode into camp as their commander. After performing ably at Spotsylvania, he was promoted to the "temporary" rank of lieutenant general.

Anderson did an able job with the First Corps until James Longstreet returned to retake his post. This shunted Anderson into command of the newly created Fourth Corps which was little more than a division in strength. Anderson's military career came to an end at Sayler's Creek on 6 April 1865 after Lee's retreat from Richmond. There his force was completely captured, but he managed to elude capture, but only to become a general without a command. Lee's army surrendered days later and Anderson returned to South Carolina to build a life in the postwar South.

The warrior found his postwar life one of tribulation. He found it hard to attain a high position, working as a clerk and a phosphate agent. Unable to retrieve his fortunes, Anderson died penniless in 1879.

CHAPTER XI

Soldiers on Parade

19-21 May 1864

*E*well's thwarted 19 May probe only briefly delayed Grant's next bold advance south. At 2200 that night, the lieutenant general notified Halleck that he would not move the army until the enemy's intentions and the threat he posed to supply wagons at Fredericksburg was divined. The next day revealed that no major threat existed and the *Army of the Potomac* could begin its march only under the cover of darkness and finally leave Spotsylvania behind for future fields of opportunity.

During 20 May, the army reordered itself once again for the night's operation, with Birney's and Tyler's troops being withdrawn and returned to Hancock on the Union left. Hancock was told he was to follow the original plan laid out the day before with the object of Milford Station and the Mattapony. The rest of the army had its marching orders as well. Torbert's cavalry division, left behind by Sheridan to help the army in his absence, was to precede Hancock's move to Milford Station. Warren was to start out in the morning to Massaponax Church and then south via the Telegraph Road to cross the Po at Stannard's Mill, establishing a bridge there for crossing to the other side. Burnside's *IX Corps* was to follow the *V Corps'* path while the *VI Corps* would follow Hancock's route.

Whether so many senior officers stood together at one time or not, Union generals standing in the rain with a battlefield covered with bodies became an enduring image of Spotsylvania.

When night finally came, Federal forces did get on the move, though the operation did not go completely smoothly and was slightly reminiscent of the movement to the Wilderness days before. Hancock stepped off around 2300, reaching Massaponax Church where he encountered Torbert's cavalry division just preparing to get underway. After a delay, the troops were on the march again by 0130 of 21 May. Warren faced the biggest problem, receiving a last minute change to his march at 0945; instead of going to the Po at Stannard's Mill via the Telegraph Road, now he was to follow Hancock toward Guinea Station,

The Spotsylvania campaign was the beginning of Meade's and Grant's dissatisfaction with General Gouverneur K. Warren, which finally led to his removal in the spring of 1865.

turning southwest to reach the river at Guinea Bridge. At 1000 he was on his way. Burnside waited for the *V Corps* to clear the way, before he followed its path south. Wright's job was to cover the army's movement, a duty that led to a brisk brief afternoon skirmish after the curious Rebels launched a probe by Wilcox's division. The enemy was turned back and Wright was free to take up his part in the march, moving out between 2000 and 2100.

The move of the *Army of the Potomac* was no great surprise to the Army of Northern Virginia. Indeed, Union deciphering of Confederate signal traffic revealed the fact that the enemy had in fact detected the advance. Fortunately for the Confederates, Lee's army would be in stronger shape for their next confrontation. A.P. Hill had returned from illness and taken back his old Third Corps' reins of command. Better still was word of rein-

General Winfield S. Hancock emerged from the Spotsylvania campaign with his reputation intact, and even enhanced.

forcements freed up by Confederate victories at Bermuda Hundred and in the Shenandoah, 1,200 men of Hoke's Brigade under Colonel William B. Lewis, 6,000 men of Brigadier General Robert F. Hoke's division, 2,500 men under Major General John C. Breckinridge's command. Still, Lee had to pursue Grant to stop him and this meant getting his army between the Federal general and Richmond. First, at 1200 on 21 May, he had Ewell get his troops on the march to Hanover Junction, to be followed later by Anderson. By nightfall, it was clear the entire Federal army was on the move and there was no reason to maintain a force at Spotsylvania. Shortly after dark, Hill's corps was on the way south as well.

With both armies marching their way south, the grim fighting at Spotsylvania finally ended. All that had really been accomplished there was some of the hardest fighting of the war, bitter face to face contests marked by furious gunfire in horrendous weather conditions. And for what basically appeared to be a grim stalemate. However, the battles of Spotsylvania did have a larger meaning which may not have been so readily apparent to the participants at the time, the unyielding determination of two men and two armies.

On the Confederate side, the Army of Northern Virginia performed almost flawlessly, making a speedy march on the 8 May to reach the battlefield at Laurel Hill, fending off Union attempts to occupy Spotsylvania Court House and continue their march. Once there, they laid formidable fortifications almost incapable of being breached, and even when they were, the army's divisions and brigades preformed with an uncanny clockwork synchronization to drive the enemy back and seal the gaps that had been made. It could be said that at Spotsylvania, the Army of Northern Virginia was operating at peak performance.

So too was its commander. His clear thinking and perception allowed him to get troops to Spotsylvania to block his enemy's move. Once there, he parried each of Grant's attempts to flank his forces and saw to the destruction of every head-on attack against his line. Of course, his misinterpretation of Grant's intentions on 11 May drew guns away from the imperiled salient and allowed the destruction of Johnson's Division, but that mistake was dwarfed by the influence Lee wielded over his subordinates in getting them to do the almost impossible.

At the same time, the *Army of the Potomac* constantly provided a worthy adversary to its Confederate counterpart. No one on the Union side could point to a lasting advantage won on the fields at Spotsylvania. Still, the Federals operated by making herculean efforts under the hot Virginia May sun and the drenching rains of that week, either maneuvering on the Confederate front or making head-on attacks. Constantly, its ranks were asked for great sacrifices and its casualty lists show that a heavy price was exacted for their efforts. Despite the lack of success though, there was now a feeling in the army that they were not being wasted, that these battles and fights were leading up to something greater. This perception was strengthened by their continual moves south toward the Confederate capital.

Their leadership certainly was competent, but in no way comparable to that which they faced. Grant and Meade were able leaders in their own right, yet at Spotsylvania their dual command structure continued to prove unwieldy, leading to conflicting orders, as in the case of the movements of the *II Corps* in the 10 May attacks and the inability to use Burnside's detached command to good use. And then there was Grant's continued folly in believing the Confederates were one step away from disaster, which he should have realized was disproved by the Confederate repulses of his pounding attacks. Grant may have been ignorant and overly optimistic, but he doggedly seized and maintained the initiative. Even when he was defeated, his determination to remain active left the enemy ill able to take advantage of their good fortune. The very fact that Lee's only offensive during the entire campaign was Ewell's feeble effort of 19 May was proof of that.

If both armies and commanders were tested on the field of Spotsylvania, both came away with their fighting qualities intact and with determination to continue the battles on other fields throughout Virginia. Spotsylvania, for all its bloody glory, proved that the Civil War would go on only until one of the opponents was fought out and could continue the contest no more.

The Butcher's Bill
A Comparison between Grant's Overland Campaign and Those of His Predecessors

Grant's reputation as merely a warrior of attrition driving up casualties by pummeling the enemy's position is undeserved. In actuality, the battles the *Army of the Potomac* fought under his direction were no bloodier than those of any of his predecessors, McDowell, McClellan, Burnside, Hooker and Meade. Grant's butcher's bill came at a higher price because he fought more battles. Consider the following table which lists the casualties of the *Army of the Potomac* from its combined major battles under its commanders and Grant's direction of the force while general in chief.

Army of the Potomac

Commander	Total Bat. Cas.	Avg. Cas.[1]	Total KIA & WIA[2]	Total MIA[3]
Irvin McDowell	2,700	9%	1,490(55%)	1,220(45%)
George B. McClellan				
John Pope	16,060	21%	10,100(63%)	5,960(37%)
Ambrose Burnside	12,650	12%	10,880(86%)	1,770(14%)
Joseph Hooker	16,800	17%	11,120(66%)	5,680(34%)
George Meade	24,700	16%	18,950(77%)	5,750(23%)
Ulysses S. Grant	84,930	13%	51,830(71%)	13,930(19%)

[1] Percentage of forces engaged.

[2] Number of MIA, WIA, & WIA for Spotsylvania 10 May 1864 and Petersburg June 15-18 1864 is not known and excluded from count.

[3] When known.

A good comparison with Lee is hard to make. For the time that the two best generals on either side faced each other, most Confederate casualty records are incomplete or non-existent. But an averaging of Lee's campaigns and battles for which we do have information reveals that Lee, not Grant, was actually more given to attrition than Grant, an activity he was ill equipped to maintain given the smaller numbers he could muster to fill out his ranks.

Anatomy of Battle
Wounds During the Battle of Spotsylvania

Much has been made of the fact that during the battlefield combat at Spotsylvania on 12 May that fighting was on many occasions nearly face to face for hours. Many soldiers recount that during the battle the bayonet was "freely used" and why not? since it would appear readily useful in the frequent episodes of charges and hand-to-hand combat that took place during the fighting. Reports on the wounds suffered by Union troops in the *Army of the Potomac* show, however, that if a soldier were to fall at Spotsylvania, it would most likely be from rifle fire.

Type of Wound	Corps II	Corps V	VI	Total
Bayonet	8	3	3	14
Bullet	3,728	3,088	1,413	8,218
Cannon Shot	21	15	1	37
Shell	214	459	39	712
Sword	0	0	1	1

Incredibly, only a handful of men suffered from bayonet wounds during the entire Spotsylvania campaign, making it no wonder that many soldiers found better use from the bayonet as a candlestick holder rather than as a battlefield weapon. (Regrettably, it is not known how many Union troops might have suffered wounds from Confederate Colonel Robert Taylor who is known to have defended himself on 10 May with a frying pan.) At the same time, the overwhelming number of casualties suffered from bullet wounds points to the domination of the bullet on the Civil War battlefield and a notable example of the conflict as being a modern war.

Arlington National Cemetery

Across the Potomac from Civil War Washington was a disturbing symbol of the continued Southern resistance against Northern attempts to restore the Union, the Arlington estate, a home of the Confederacy's greatest general, Robert E. Lee. The prize land, 1,100 acres, and handsome mansion were originally owned by George Washington Parke

Custis, a gentleman with a close, if not confusing, connection to the nation's first president; he was both George Washington's adopted son and grandson to Martha Washington by her first marriage. Custis' only child, Mary, married then Second Lieutenant Lee in 1831.

After George Custis died in 1857, the property passed into Mary Lee's hands to be held by her until it could be passed on to her eldest son, George Washington Custis Lee. The events of the Civil War eventually forced the Lees to abandon Arlington forever, the property later being occupied by Union troops as a camp and headquarters. The government seized the property under the pretext of the Lees' failure to pay taxes.

As casualties continued to mount and the death toll rose, especially during Grant's campaigns of 1864, a need arose in Washington for a place to bury the war dead. Arlington's prominent location made it ideal for a cemetery. Lincoln consented to making the estate a final resting place for soldiers at Stanton's urging. The first soldier to be buried there was Private William Christman of the *67th Pennsylvania Infantry* on 13 May.

Since the Civil War American soldiers and sailors have continued to be buried at Arlington. Some more prominent names of those interred there include General John J. Pershing, Admiral Richard Byrd, President William H. Taft, General George C. Marshall, William Jennings Bryan and President John F. Kennedy, his wife Jacqueline, and brother Robert. The cemetery is also site to the tomb of the unknown soldier.

Order of Battle

SPOTSYLVANIA

UNION FORCES
Lieut. Gen. Ulysses S. Grant

Unit	KIA	WIA	MIA	Total
GENERAL HQ				
Escort				
5th U.S. Cav.	-	-	-	-

ARMY OF THE POTOMAC*
Maj. Gen. George Gordon Meade

Unit	KIA	WIA	MIA	Total
Provost Guard				
Brig. Gen Marsena Patrick				
1st Mass. Cav. Cos. C and D	-	-	-/3	3
80th N.Y. Inf.	-	-	-	-
3d Pa. Cav.	-	-	-	-
68th Pa. Inf.	-	-/3	-	3
114th Pa Inf.	-	-	-	-
Total	-	-/3	-/3	6
Engineer Troops				
50th N.Y.	-	-	-	-
Battalion U.S.	-	-	-	-
Total	-	-	-	-
Guards and Orderlies				
Ind. Co,. Oneida Cav.	-	-	-/2	-
Total	-	-	-/2	2

---

* Cavalry Corp absent on expedition toward from 9 May. Reserve
artillery ordered to Washington 16 May.

Unit	KIA	WIA	MIA	Total

II ARMY CORPS
Maj. Gen. Winfield Scott Hancock

Unit	KIA	WIA	MIA	Total
Staff	-	2/-	-	-
1st Vermont Cav., Co. M	-	-	-	-
Total	-	2/-	-	2

FIRST DIVISION
Brig. Gen. Francis C. Barlow

First Brigade
Col. Nelson C. Miles

Unit	KIA	WIA	MIA	Total
Staff	-	1/-	-	1
20th Michigan	-/35	6/115	-/11	167
61st N.Y.	2/19	5/74	-/2	102
81st Pa.	1/9	2/61	-/4	77
140th Pa.	-/34	6/120	-/9	169
183d Pa.	2/16	2/107	1/33	161
Total	5/113	22/477	1/59	677

Second Brigade
Col. Thomas A. Smyth*
Col. Richard Byrnes

Unit	KIA	WIA	MIA	Total
28th Massachusetts	2/21	3/76	/8	110
63d N.Y.	1/5	-/22	-/3	31
69th N.Y.	1/16	3/79	-/23	122
88th N.Y.	-/2	-/20	-/3	25
118th Pa.	1/7	2/50	-/30	90
Total	5/51	8/247	-/67	378

Third Brigade
Col. Paul Frank
Col. Hiram L. Brown**
Col. Clinton D. McDougall

Unit	KIA	WIA	MIA	Total
Staff	-	1/-	-	1
39th N.Y.	1/13	9/83	1/25	132
52d N.Y.***	2/19	9/106	-/28	164

---

* Assigned to command Third Brigade, Second Division, 17 May.
** Assigned 10 May, captured 12 May.
*** Detachment 7th New York Attached

Unit	KIA	WIA	MIA	Total
57th N.Y.*	-	-	-	-
111th N.Y.	-/12	4/33	-/13	62
125th N.Y.	2/8	3/74	-/6	90
126th N.Y.	2/4	5/32	-/7	50
Total	7/56	31/325	1/79	499

Fourth Brigade
Col. John R. Brooke

2d Del.	2/4	1/23	-/11	41
64th N.Y.	3/9	3/48	1/11	75
66th N.Y.	1/8	2/42	-/20	73
53d Pa.	1/25	1/122	-/28	177
145th Pa.	4/19	5/98	1/45	172
148th Pa.	-/33	10/225	-/33	301
Total	11/98	22/558	2/148	839
TOTAL FIRST DIVISION:	28/318	83/1,607	4/353	2,393

SECOND DIVISION
Brig. Gen. John Gibbon

Provost Guard

2d Co. Minn. Sharpshooters	-	-	-	-

First Brigade
Brig. Gen. Alexander Webb**
Col H. Boyd McKeen

Staff	-	1/-	-	1
19th Me.	-/11	4/60	-/9	84
15th Mass.	1/3	-/16	-/1	21
19th Mass.	1/7	-/37	1/4	50
20th Mass.	2/16	2/73	-/9	102
1st Co. Andrew Sharpshooters	-	-/3	-/3	6
7th Mi.	-/7	4/22	-/1	34
42d N.Y.	4/8	2/26	-/9	49

---

* On provost duty at Fredericksburg.
** Wounded 12 May.

Unit	KIA	WIA	MIA	Total
59th N.Y.	1/3	2/21	1/4	32
82d N.Y.	-/6	4/33	-/8	51
36th Wi.*	-	-	-	-
Total	9/61	19/291	2/48	430
Second Brigade				
Brig. Gen. Joshua T. Owen				
152d N.Y.	-/9	2/50	-/9	70
69th Pa.	1/2	3/26	-/6	38
71st Pa.	1/7	1/59	-/8	76
72d Pa.	-/4	-/22	1/12	39
106th Pa.	2/11	1/31	-/3	48
Total	4/83	7/188	1/38	271
Third Brigade				
Col. Samuel S. Carroll**				
Col. Theodore G. Ellis				
Col. Thomas A. Smyth***				
14th Ct.	-/4	1/55	-/8	68
1st Del.	-/7	5/38	-/3	53
14th Ind.	1/5	6/70	-/1	83
12th N.J.	1/13	4/71	-/9	98
10th N.Y. Battalion	1/8	2/44	-/6	61
108th N.Y.	-/4	2/40	-/7	53
4th Oh.	-/13	5/64	1/5	88
8th Oh.	1/6	7/56	-/7	77
7th W.V.	1/4	2/59	-/6	72
Total	5/64	34/497	1/52	653
Fourth Brigade**				
Col. Matthew Murphy+				
Col. James P. McIvor				
155 N.Y.	-/8	3/42	-/5	58
164th N.Y.	2/10	3/63	-/14	92
170th N.Y.	1/9	2/15	-/2	29

---

* Joined 19 May.
** Wounded, May 13
*** Assigned, May 17
**** Joined, May 17
+ Wounded, May 18

Unit	KIA	WIA	MIA	Total
182d N.Y. (99th N.Y.				
National Guard Art.)	-/4	3/20	-/3	30
Total	3/31	11/140	-/24	209
TOTAL SECOND DIVISION:	21/189	71/1,116	4/162	1,563

THIRD DIVISION
Maj. Gen. David B. Birney

Staff	-/-	2/-	-/-	2

First Brigade
Brig. Gen. J. H. Hobart Ward
Col. Thomas W. Egan*

Staff	-/-	1/-	-/-	1
20th Ind.	1/9	1/41	1/8	61
3d Me.	1/9	2/48	1/14	74
40th N.Y.	-/11	7/50	1/27	96
86th N.Y.	1/15	4/77	-/28	125
124th N.Y.	-/7	6/40	-/8	61
99th Pa.	2/5	3/47	-/6	63
110th Pa.	1/4	3/50	-/10	68
141st Pa.	-/3	2/34	-/8	47
2d U.S. Sharpshooters	-/12	3/35	-/3	53
Total	5/75	32/422	3/112	649

Second Brigade
Col. John Crocker
Col. Elijah Walker**

4th Me.	-/-	1/13	-/9	23
17th Me.	-/3	3/51	-/12	69
3d Mi.	-/1	3/51	-/12	45
5th Mi	-/5	-/44	-/9	58
93d N.Y.	-/3	2/35	1/4	45
57th Pa.	1/5	3/19	-/4	32
63d Pa.	-/1	1/21	-/12	35
105th Pa.	-/3	5/19	1/4	32

* Assigned May 12.
** Assigned, May 18

Unit	KIA	WIA	MIA	Total
1st U.S. Sharpshooters	1/4	1/18	-/1	25
Total	2/25	17/257	2/61	364
TOTAL THIRD DIVISION:	7/100	51/679	5/173	1,015

FOURTH DIVISION*
Brig. Gen. Gershom Mott

Staff	-/-	1/-	-/-	1

First Brigade
Col. Robert McAllister

	KIA	WIA	MIA	Total
Staff	1/-	-/-	-/-	1
1st Mass.	1/1	2/41	-/3	48
16th Mass.	1/4	1/28	-/2	36
5th N.J.	-/-	2/16	-/2	20
6th N.J.	-/1	6/26	-/-	33
7th N.J.	1/2	6/27	-/6	42
8th N.J.	-/-	-/4	1/2	7
11th N.J.	3/4	1/21	-/2	31
26th Pa.	1/7	1/30	-/1	40
115th Pa.	-/-	-/19	-/-	19
Total	8/19	19/212	1/18	277

Second Brigade
Col. William R. Brewster

	KIA	WIA	MIA	Total
11th Mass.	-/5	2/33	-/4	44
70th N.Y.	-/2	2/29	-/10	43
71st N.Y.	-/3	1/11	-/2	17
72d N.Y.	-/1	3/27	-/9	40
73d N.Y.	3/3	2/20	-/2	30
74th N.Y.	1/2	1/11	-/1	16
120th N.Y.	-/-	-/10	-/2	12
8th Pa.	-/8	1/27	-/1	37
Total	4/24	12/108	-/31	239
TOTAL FOURTH DIVISION:	12/43	32/380	1/49	517

---

* Assigned as the Third and Fourth Brigades of the Third Division May 13, Mott taking command of the former and Brewster of the latter brigade. All losses from 8 May to 21 May are given without regard to this change in organization.

Unit	KIA	WIA	MIA	Total

Fourth Division Heavy Artillery*
Brig. Gen. Robert O. Tyler

Unit	KIA	WIA	MIA	Total
1st Maine Hvy Art.	5/75	7/388	-/5	481
1st Mass. Hvy Art.	2/48	17/295	-/28	390
2d N.Y. Hvy. Art.	1/16	8/95	1/1	117
7th N.Y. Hvy. Art.	2/7	2/58	-/7	58
8th N.Y. Hvy. Art.	-/8	1/20	-/4	33
Total Fourth Division Heavy Artillery	10/155	30/856	1/45	1,097

Artillery Brigade
Col. John C. Tidball

Unit	KIA	WIA	MIA	Total
Staff	-/-	1/-	-/-	1
Maine Lt., 6th Bat. (F)	-/1	1/1	-/-	3
Mass. Lt., 10th Bat.	-/1	-/1	-/-	2
1st N.H. Lt., 1st Bat. B**	-/-	1/2	-/-	3
1st N.J., Lt. Bat. G	-/2	-/6	-/-	8
4th N.Y. Hvy., 3d Bat.	-/-	-/1	-/1	2
N.Y. Lt., 11th Bat.***	-/-	-/-	-/-	-
N.Y. Lt., 12th Bat.****	-/-	-/-	-/3	3
1st Pa. Lt., Bat. F	-/-	-/-	-/-	-
1st R.I. Lt., Bat. A	-/1	-/2	-/-	3
1st R.I. Lt., Bat. B	-/4	1/3	-/-	8
4th U.S., Bat. K	-/1	-/4	-/-	5
5th U.S., Bats. C and I	-/1	1/14	-/-	15
Total	-/11	5/35	-/4	55
TOTAL II ARMY CORPS:	78/816	274/4,673	15/786	6,642

---

* Joined 18 and 19 May .
** Transferred frpm Artillery Reserve May 16.
*** Transferred from Artillery Reserve 16 May.
**** Transferred from Artillery Reserve 16 May.

Unit	KIA	WIA	MIA	Total

V ARMY CORPS
Maj. Gen. Gouverneur K. Warren

Unit	KIA	WIA	MIA	Total
Staff	-/-	1/-	-/-	1
Provost Guard	-/-	-/-	-/-	-

FIRST DIVISION
Brig. Gen. Charles Griffin

First Brigade
Brig. Gen. Romney B. Ayres

Unit	KIA	WIA	MIA	Total
140th N.Y.	2/10	3/45	-/-	60
146th N.Y.	-/3	1/12	-/-	16
91st Pa.	-/9	3/60	-/-	72
155th Pa.	1/7	-/51	-/2	61
2d U.S.	-/12	4/30	-/3	49
11th U.S.	-/17	1/100	-/10	128
12th U.S.	-/3	5/22	-/25	65
14th U.S.	-/12	3/83	-/-	98
17th U.S.	-/13	5/58	-/4	80
Total	3/86	25/471	-/44	629

Second Brigade
Col. Jacob B. Sweitzer

Unit	KIA	WIA	MIA	Total
9th Mass.	2/23	3/68	-/9	105
22d Mass.*	1/17	-/52	-/9	79
32d Mass.	-/23	5/96	-/5	129
4th Mich.	-/5	1/28	-/4	38
62d Pa.	1/13	5/107	-/18	144
Total	4/81	14/351	-/45	405

Third Brigade
Brig. Gen. Joseph J. Bartlett

Unit	KIA	WIA	MIA	Total
20th Me.	1/7	3/18	-/2	31
18th Mass.	-/1	-/14	-/1	16
1st Mi.	1/2	1/18	-/-	22
16th Mi	-/7	-/33	-/3	43
44th N.Y.	-/8	3/52	-/9	72
83d Pa.	2/19	4/115	-/24	164

* 2d Co. Mass. Sharpshooters attached.

Unit	KIA	WIA	MIA	Total
118th Pa.	-/9	2/29	-/2	42
Total	4/53	13/279	-/41	390
TOTAL FIRST DIVISION:	11/220	52/1,101	-/130	1,514

SECOND DIVISION*
Brig. Gen. James Robinson**

Staff	-/-	1/-	-/-	-

First Brigade
Col. Peter Lyle

16th Me.	-/13	9/110	-/11	143
13th Mass.	1/1	1/23	1/18	45
39th Mass.	1/18	6/115	-/28	168
104th N.Y.	-/5	1/36	-/4	46
90th Pa.	1/6	2/42	-/3	54
107th Pa.***	-/-	-/1	1/-	2
Total	3/43	19/327	2/64	458

Second Brigade
Col. Richard Coulter****

12th Mass.	2/14	3/29	-/1	49
83d N.Y. (9th Militia)	2/27	6/88	-/5	128
97th N.Y.	-/6	2/65	-/2	75
11th Pa.	1/9	2/97	-/3	112
88th Pa.	-/14	3/62	-/2	81
Total	5/70	16/341	-/13	445

---

* On 9 May, the division was temporarily disbanded. The First Brigade was attached to the Fourth Division, the Second to the Third Division, and the Third Brigade served as an indepedent command under direct orders of the corps commander. This arrangement continued until 30 May.

** Wounded 8 May.

*** Joined 16 May.

**** Coulter assumed division command from 8 May - 9 May. He was succeeded in brigade command by Bates during this time. When Coulter was wounded on 19 May, Bates again took brigade command.

Unit	KIA	WIA	MIA	Total
Third Brigade				
Col. Andrew W. Denison*				
Col. Charles E. Phelps**				
Col. Richard N. Bowerman				
1st Md.	-/10	6/58	-/20	94
4th Md.	1/2	2/40	-/7	52
7th Md.	-/6	2/41	2/10	61
8th Md.	1/5	3/35	-/43	50
Total	2/23	13/174	2/43	257
TOTAL SECOND DIVISION:	10/136	49/842	4/120	1,161

THIRD DIVISION
Brig. Gen. Samuel W. Crawford

Unit	KIA	WIA	MIA	Total
First Brigade				
Col. William McCandless***				
Col. William C. Talley****				
Col. Wellington H. Ent				
Col. Samuel M. Jackson				
Col. Martin D. Hartin+				
1st Pa. Reserves	-/6	2/73	2/13	96
2d Pa. Reserves	-/3	3/20	-/1	27
6th Pa. Reserves	1/9	1/38	1/4	54
7th Pa. Reserves	-/-	-/2	-/-	2
11th Pa. Reserves	-/1	-/7	-/1	9
13th Pa. Reserves	1/14	5/59	-/2	81
Total	2/33	11/199	3/21	269
Third Brigade				
Col. Joseph Fisher				
5th Pa. Reserves	-/9	2/17	1/2	31
8th Pa. Reserves++	1/6	4/49	-/5	65
10th Pa. Reserves	-/9	-/24	-/12	45

---

   * Wounded 8 May.
  ** Wounded and captured 8 May.
 *** Wounded 8 May.
**** Captured 8 May.
   + Assumed command 18 May.
 ++ Left army 15 May.

Unit	KIA	WIA	MIA	Total
12th Pa. Reserves	-/7	-/16	-/2	25
Total	1/31	6/106	1/21	166
TOTAL THIRD DIVISION:	3/64	17/305	4/42	435

FOURTH DIVISION
Brig. Gen. Lysander Cutler

First Brigade
Col. William W. Robinson

Unit	KIA	WIA	MIA	Total
7th Ind.	1/8	3/35	-/-	47
19th Ind.	-/6	2/31	-/-	52
24th Mi.	-/20	2/37	-/1	60
1st Batt. N.Y. Sharpshooters	-/1	2/11	-/-	14
2d Wi.*	1/1	-/2	-/2	6
6th Wi.	2/8	3/65	-/5	83
7th Wi.	-/19	1/57	-/3	80
Total	4/63	13/238	-/11	329

Second Brigade
Brig. Gen. James C. Rice**
Col. Edward B. Fowler***
Col. J. William Hofmann

Unit	KIA	WIA	MIA	Total
Staff	1/-	-/-	-/-	1
76th N.Y.	-/7	1/41	-/3	52
84th N.Y. (14th Militia)	1/12	6/99	-/5	123
95th N.Y.	-/6	2/49	-/8	65
147th N.Y.	-/8	2/30	-/3	43
56th Pa.	-/6	1/28	-/1	36
Total	2/39	12/247	-/20	320

Third Brigade
Col. Edward S. Bragg

Unit	KIA	WIA	MIA	Total
121st Pa.	1/6	-/16	-/-	23
142d Pa.	-/4	-/19	-/8	31
143d Pa.	1/15	2/52	-/3	73
149th Pa.	1/11	3/81	-/3	99

---

* Provost guard of division from 11 May.
** Killed 10 May.
*** Relieved 21 May.

Unit	KIA	WIA	MIA	Total
150th Pa.	-/7	2/41	-/1	51
Total	3/43	7/209	-/15	277
TOTAL FOURTH DIVISION:	9/145	32/694	-/46	926

Heavy Artillery Brigade*
Col. J. Howard Kitching

6th N.Y.	-/18	6/125	-/12	161
15th N.Y. (1st and 3d Batts.)	-/18	1/131	1/5	156
Total	-/36	7/236	1/17	317

Artillery Brigade
Col. Charles S. Wainwright

Mass. Lt., 3d Batty. (C)	-/-	1/6	-/-	7
Mass. Lt., 5th Batty. (E)	-/2	-/3	-/-	5
Mass. Lt., 9th Batty.**	-/-	-/-	-/-	-
1st N.Y. Lt., Batty. B***	-/-	-/-	-/-	-
1st N.Y. Lt., Batty. C****	-/-	-/-	-/-	-
1st N.Y. Lt., Batty. D	-/-	-/4	-/-	4
1st N.Y. Lt., Batts. E and L	-/2	-/2	-/-	4
1st N.Y. Lt., 5th Batty.+	-/3	-/1	-/3	7
1st N.Y. Lt., 15th Batty.++	-/-	-/-	-/1	1
4th U.S., Batty. B	-/3	1/6	-/-	10
5th U.S., Batty. D	-/1	-/2	-/-	3
Total	-/23	5/87	-/11	126
TOTAL V ARMY CORPS	33/624	163/3,285	9/366	4,486

---

* Transferred from Artillery Reserve 13 May.

** Transferred from the Artillery Reserve 16 May. The 5th New York Battery was sent to Washington 19 May.

*** Transferred from the Artillery Reserve 16 May. The 5th New York Battery was sent to Washington 19 May.

**** Transferred from the Artillery Reserve 16 May. The 5th New York Battery was sent to Washington 19 May.

+ Transferred from the Artillery Reserve 16 May. The 5th New York Battery was sent to Washington 19 May.

++ Transferred from the Artillery Reserve 16 May. The 5th New York Battery was sent to Washington 19 May.

Unit	KIA	WIA	MIA	Total

VI ARMY CORPS
Maj. Gen. John Sedgwick*
Brig. Gen. Horatio G. Wright

Unit	KIA	WIA	MIA	Total
Staff	1/-	-/-	-/-	-
Escort				
8th Pa. Cav., Co. A	-/-	-/-	-/-	-

FIRST DIVISION
Brig. Gen. Horatio G. Wright
Brig. Gen. David A. Russell

First Brigade
Col. Henry W. Brown
Col. William H. Penrose

Unit	KIA	WIA	MIA	Total
Staff	-/-	-/-	-/1	-
1st N.J.	1/2	2/48	1/8	62
2d N.J.	1/3	1/36	1/26	68
3d N.J.	1/19	6/92	1/29	148
4th N.J.	-/15	4/62	2/6	89
10th N.J.	-/15	2/78	5/49	149
15 N.J.	4/71	2/157	2/36	272
Total	7/125	17/473	15/154	789

Second Brigade
Col. Emory Upton

Unit	KIA	WIA	MIA	Total
5th Me.	1/16	14/81	1/18	131
121st N.Y.	3/46	9/97	-/-	155
95th Pa.	-/26	3/79	-/27	135
96th Pa.	-/31	6/109	-/32	178
Total	4/119	32/366	1/77	599

Third Brigade
Brig. Gen. David A. Russell
Brig. Gen. Henry L. Eustis

Unit	KIA	WIA	MIA	Total
Staff	-/-	1/-	-/-	1
6th Me.	3/8	7/96	-/21	139
49th Pa.	3/47	12/168	-/44	274

---

* KIA 9 May.

Unit	KIA	WIA	MIA	Total
119th Pa.	3/28	1/88	-/25	145
5th Wis.	2/17	5/97	-/28	149
Total	11/100	26/449	-/118	704

Fourth Brigade
Col. Nelson Cross

	KIA	WIA	MIA	Total
65th N.Y.	1/19	2/45	1/28	97
67th N.Y.	3/15	-/28	-/2	48
122d N.Y.	-/-	-/20	1/3	24
82d Pa. (detachment)	-/1	-/1	-/-	2
Total	4/35	2/95	2/33	171

TOTAL FIRST DIVISION: 26/379   77/1,383   16/382   2,263

SECOND DIVISION
Brig. Gen. Thomas H. Neill

	KIA	WIA	MIA	Total
Staff	-/-	-/1	-/-	1

First Brigade
Brig. Gen. Frank Wheaton

	KIA	WIA	MIA	Total
62d N.Y.	-/2	1/9	-/-	12
93d Pa.	-/9	2/68	-/-	79
98th Pa.	-/2	-/18	-/-	20
102d Pa.	-/5	1/38	-/-	41
139th Pa.	-/12	3/100	-/1	116
Total	-/30	7/233	-/1	271

Second Brigade
Brig. Gen. Lewis A. Grant

	KIA	WIA	MIA	Total
1st Vt. (Hvy. Arty.)*	-/2	2/21	-/-	25
2d Vt.	-/27	5/75	-/16	123
3d Vt.	-/21	1/52	-/-	74
4th Vt.	-/5	-/37	-/-	42
5th Vt.	-/8	2/58	-/7	75
6th Vt.	-/8	1/28	-/-	37
Total	-/71	11/271	-/23	376

---

* Joined 14 May.

Unit	KIA	WIA	MIA	Total
Third Brigade				
Col. Daniel D. Bidwell				
Staff	-/-	1/-	-/-	1
7th Maine	2/18	14/83	-/9	126
43d N.Y.	-/-	3/35	1/12	51
49th N.Y.	4/20	5/84	1/17	131
77th N.Y.	2/9	5/65	3/23	107
61st N.Y.	1/30	6/96	-/6	139
Total	9/77	34/363	5/67	565
Fourth Brigade				
Brig. Gen. Henry I. Eustis				
Col. Oliver O. Edwards				
71st Mass.	1/1	-/10	-/9	14
10th Mass.	1/14	10/54	-/13	92
37th Mass.	-/16	9/56	-/10	91
2d R.I.	1/14	2/30	-/6	53
Total	5/45	21/150	-/31	250
TOTAL SECOND DIVISION:	12/223	74/1,017	5/122	1,453

THIRD DIVISION
Brig. Gen. James Ricketts

Unit	KIA	WIA	MIA	Total
First Brigade				
Brig. Gen. William H. Morris*				
Col. John W. Schall				
Col. William S. Truex**				
Staff	-/-	1/-	-/-	1
14th N.J.	-/4	-/24	-/-	28
106th N.J.	1/5	1/31	-/-	38
151st N.Y.	-/2	-/20	-/1	23
87th Pa.	-/1	-/32	-/2	35
10th Vt.	-/2	1/21	-/-	24
Total	1/14	3/128	-/3	149

---

* Wounded 9 May.
** Assumed command 14 May.

Unit	KIA	WIA	MIA	Total
Second Brigade				
Col. Benjamin F. Smith				
6th Md.	1/1	-/4	-/-	6
110th Ohio	-/4	2/28	-/-	34
122d Ohio	-/1	1/10	-/-	12
126th Ohio	1/20	-/56	-/1	78
67th Pa.	-/1	-/12	-/2	15
138th Pa.	-/1	-/11	-/-	12
Total	2/28	3/121	-/3	157
TOTAL THIRD DIVISION:	3/42	6/249	-/6	306

Artillery Brigade
Col. Charles H. Tompkins

Unit	KIA	WIA	MIA	Total
Me. Lt., 4th Batty. (D)	-/-	-/-	-/-	-
Me. Lt., 5th Batty. (E)*	-/-	-/-	-/-	-
Mass. Lt., 1st Batty. (A)	-/-	1/1	-/-	2
1st N.J. Lt. Batty. A**	-/-	-/-	-/2	2
N.Y. Lt., 1st Batty.	-/-	-/3	-/1	4
N.Y. Lt., 3rd Batty.	-/1	-/-	-/-	1
4th N.Y. Hvy. (1st Batt.)	-/-	-/3	-/-	3
1st Ohio Light, Batty. H***	-/-	-/-	-/-	-
1st R.I. Lt., Batty. C	-/-	-/-	-/-	-
1st R.I. Lt., Batty. E	-/-	-/1	-/-	1
1st R.I. Lt., Batty. G	-/-	-/-	-/-	-
5th U.S., Batty. E****	-/-	-/-	-/-	-
5th U.S., Batty. M	-/1	-/5	-/-	6

Artillery
Brig. Gen. Henry Hunt

Second Brigade Horse Arty.
Capt. Dunbar Ransom

Unit	KIA	WIA	MIA	Total
1st U.S., Batts. E and G	-/-	-/-	-/-	-
1st U.S., Batts. H and I	-/-	-/-	-/-	-

---

* Transferred from the Artillery Reserve 16 May,
** Transferred from Artillery Reserve 16 May.
*** Transferred from the Artillery Reserve 16 May.
**** Transferred from Artillery Reserve 16 May.

Unit	KIA	WIA	MIA	Total
1st U.S., Batty. K	-/-	-/-	-/-	-
2d U.S., Batty. A	-/-	-/-	-/-	-
2d U.S., Batty. G	-/-	-/-	-/-	-
3d U.S., U.S. Batts. C, F, K	-/-	-/-	-/-	-

Artillery Park
Lt. Col. Freeman McGilvery

| 15th N.Y. Hvy. Arty. (2d Batty.) | -/- | -/4 | -/- | - |

Unattached Cavalry

| 22d N.Y. | -/- | -/3 | 2/72 | - |

TOTAL
ARMY OF THE POTOMAC:

| | 153/2,086 | 595/10,630 | 47/1,742 | 15,253 |

IX ARMY CORPS
Maj. Gen. Ambrose Burnside

| Staff | -/- | 1/- | -/- | - |

Provost Guard

| 8th U.S. Infantry | -/- | -/- | -/- | - |

FIRST DIVISION
Brig. Gen. Thomas G. Stevenson*
Col. Daniel Leasure
Maj. Daniel L. Crittendon**

| Staff | 1/- | -/- | -/- | - |

First Brigade
Col. Jacob Gould***
Lt. Col. Stephen M. Weld, Jr.
Brig. Gen. James H. Ledlie****

35th Mass.	-/3	2/13	-/1	19
56th Mass.	-/14	4/95	-/5	119
57th Mass.	-/17	3/68	-/27	115

---

* KIA 10 May.
** Assumed command 12 May.
*** Disabled by sickness 8 May.
**** Assumed command 13 May.

Unit	KIA	WIA	MIA	Total
59th Mass.	1/10	-/49	-/5	63
4th U.S.	-/4	-/6	-/10	20
10th U.S.	-/2	1/8	-/-	11
Total	1/50	10/240	-/45	347

Second Brigade
Col. Daniel Leasure*

Lt. Col. Gilbert P. Robinson
Col. Daniel Leasure**
Lt. Col. Gilbert P. Robinson

Unit	KIA	WIA	MIA	Total
3d Md.	1/2	1/24	-/1	29
21st Mass.	-/3	1/34	-/1	39
100th Pa.	-/23	1/109	-/2	135
Total	1/28	3/167	-/4	203

Provisional Brigade*
Col. Elisha G. Marshall

Unit	KIA	WIA	MIA	Total
2d N.Y. Mounted Rifles (Dismounted)	-/-	-/3	1/-	4
14th N.Y.	-/8	-/43	-/3	54
24th N.Y. Mounted Rifles (Dismounted)	-/-	2/6	-/2	10
2d Pa. Prov. Hvy. Arty.	-/1	-/2	-/1	4
Total	-/9	2/54	1/6	72

Artillery

Unit	KIA	WIA	MIA	Total
Me. Lt., 2d Batty. (B)	-/-	1/4	-/-	5
Mass. Lt., 14th Batty.	-/-	-/5	-/-	5
Total	-/-	1/9	-/-	10
TOTAL FIRST DIVISION:	3/87	16/470	1/56	638

---

* Commanded the division 10-12 May.
** Disabled by sickness 14 May.
*** Discontinued as an unattached command and assigned to the First Division 12 May.

Unit	KIA	WIA	MIA	Total

SECOND DIVISION
Brig. Gen. Robert B. Potter

First Brigade
Col. John I. Curtin

Unit	KIA	WIA	MIA	Total
36th Mass.	2/20	1/59	-/2	184
58th Mass.	2/15	4/72	-/5	105
51st N.Y.	-/11	-/32	-/-	43
45th Pa.	-/6	1/66	-/3	76
48th Pa.	1/16	1/85	-/-	103
7th R.I.	-/13	3/46	-/-	62
Total	5/81	10/387	-/10	473

Second Brigade
Col. Simon Griffin

Unit	KIA	WIA	MIA	Total
2d Md. (detachment)	-/6	-/7	-/13	36
31st Me.	1/10	-/94	-/1	106
32d Me.	1/12	3/41	-/-	57
6th N.H.	-/7	2/66	-/1	76
9th N.H.	1/40	5/90	1/47	184
11th N.H.	-/10	3/82	-/5	100
17th Vt.	-/10	3/57	-/-	70
Total	3/95	16/437	1/67	619

Artillery

Unit	KIA	WIA	MIA	Total
Mass. Lt., 11th Batt.	-/-	-/2	-/-	2
N.Y. Lt., 19th Batt.	-/7	-/9	-/-	16
Total	-/7	-/11	-/-	18

	KIA	WIA	MIA	Total
TOTAL SECOND DIVISION:	8/183	26/815	1/77	1,110

THIRD DIVISION
Brig. Gen. Orlando B. Willcox

First Brigade
Col. John F. Hartranft

Unit	KIA	WIA	MIA	Total
2d Mi.	1/1	1/9	-/-	12
8th Mi.	-/9	4/44	-/-	57
17th Mi.	2/20	1/33	7/89	152
27th Mi*	-/30	4/152	-/9	195
109 N.Y.	1/24	3/83	-/29	140

Unit	KIA	WIA	MIA	Total
51st Pa.	1/7	3/88	2/30	131
Total	5/91	16/409	9/157	687
Second Brigade				
Col. Benjamin C. Christ				
Col. William Humphrey*				
1st Mi. Sharpshooters	1/37	6/115	-/3	162
20th Mi.	4/13	3/105	-/19	144
79th N.Y.**	-/3	1/12	-/-	16
60th Oh.***	-/22	4/55	-/8	89
Total	5/98	18/392	2/140	656
Artillery				
Me. Lt., 7th Batt. (G)	-/2	-/3	-/-	5
N.Y. Lt., 34th Batt.	-/-	-/2	-/-	2
Total	-/2	-/5	-/-	7
TOTAL THIRD DIVISION:	10/191	34/806	12/297	1,350

FOURTH DIVISION****

Unit	KIA	WIA	MIA	Total
23rd U.S.C.T.	-/-	-/2	-/-	2
Cavalry				
3d N.J.	-/3	-/7	-/10	20
5th N.Y.	-/1	-/6	1/8	16
2d Ohio	-/-	-/7	-/6	13
13th Pa.	-/-	-/1	-/-	1
Total	-/4	-/21	1/24	50
TOTAL IX ARMY CORPS:	21/465	77/2,114	15/454	3,146
TOTAL UNION FORCES:	**174/2,551**	**672/12,744**	**62/2,196**	**18,399**

+++ 1st and 2d Cos. Mi. Sharpshooters attached.
   * Assumed command 12 May.
  ** Left army 13 May.
 *** 9th and 10th Cos. Ohio Sharpshooters attached.
**** In reserve guarding trains.

CONFEDERATE FORCES

ARMY OF NORTHERN VIRGINIA
Gen. Robert E. Lee

FIRST ARMY CORPS
Maj. Gen. Richard H. Anderson

KERSHAW'S DIVISION
 Brig. Gen. Joseph B. Kershaw

Kershaw's Brigade
 Col. John W. Henagan
  2d S.C.
  3d S.C.
  7th S.C.
  8th S.C.
  15th S.C.
  3d S.C. Battalion

Wofford's Brigade
 Brig. Gen. William T. Wofford
  16th Ga.
  18th Ga.
  24th Ga.
  Cobb's (Ga.) Legion
  Philip's (Ga.) Legion
  3d Ga. Battalion Sharpshooters

Humphrey's Brigade
 Brig. Gen. Benjamin G. Humphreys
  13th Miss.
  17th Miss.
  18th Miss.
  21st Miss.

Bryan's Brigade
  Brig. Gen. Goode Bryan
    10th Ga.
    50th Ga.
    51st Ga.
    53d Ga.

FIELD'S DIVISION
  Maj. Gen. Charles W. Field

Jenkin's Brigade
  Col. John Bratton
    1st S.C.
    2d S.C. (Rifles)
    5th S.C.
    6th S.C.
    Palmetto Sharpshooters

Anderson's Brigade
  Brig. Gen. George T. Anderson
    7th Ga.
    8th Ga.
    9th Ga.
    11th Ga.
    59th Ga.

Gregg's Brigade
  Brig. Gen. John Gregg
    3d Ark.
    1st Tex.
    4th Tex.
    5th Tex.

Benning's Brigade
  Col. Dudley M. Dubose
    2d Ga.
    15th Ga.
    17th Ga.
    20th Ga.

Law's Brigade
  Brig. Gen. E. McIvor Law
    4th Ala.

15th Ala.
44th Ala.
47th Ala.
48th Ala.

Artillery
Brig. Gen. E. Porter Alexander

Haskell's Battalion
Maj. John C. Haskell
Flanner's (N.C.) Batt.
Garden's (S.C.) Batt.
Lamkin's (Va.) Batt.
Ramsay's (N.C.) Batt.

Cabell's Battalion
Col. Henry C. Cabell
Callaway's (Ga.) Batt.
Carlton's (Ga.) Batt.
McCarthy's (Va.) Batt.
Manly's (N.C.) Batt.

Huger's Battalion
Lt. Col. Frank Huger
Fickling's (S.C.) Batt.
Moody's (La.) Batt.
Parker's (Va.) Batt.
Smith's (Va.) Batt.
Taylor's (Va.) Batt.
Woofolk's (Va.) Batt.

SECOND ARMY CORPS
Lieut. Gen. Richard S. Ewell

EARLY'S DIVISION
Brig. Gen. John B. Gordon

Pegram's Brigade
Col. John S. Hoffman
13th Va.
31st Va.
49th Va.

52d Va.
58th Va.

Gordon's Brigade
Col. Clement A. Evans

13th Ga.
26th Ga.
31st Ga.
38th Ga.
60th Ga.
61st. Ga.

Johnston's Brigade
Brig. Gen. Robert D. Johnston*

5th N.C.
12th N.C.
20th N.C.
23d N.C.

JOHNSON'S DIVISION
Maj. Gen. Edward Johnson

Stonewall Brigade
Brig. Gen. James Walker**

2d Va
4th Va.
5th Va.
27th Va.
33d Va.

Steuart's Brigade
Brig. Gen. George H. Steuart

1st N.C.
3d N.C.
10th Va.
23d Va.
37th Va.

---

* WIA, 12 May 1864
** WIA, 12 May 1864

Jones' Brigade
  Col. William Witcher

    21st Va.
    25th Va.
    42d Va.
    44th Va.
    48th Va.
    50th Va.

Louisiana Brigade (Consolidated)*
Brig. Gen. Harry T. Hays**

    1st La.
    2d La.
    5th La.
    6th La.
    7th La.
    8th La.
    9th La.
    10th La.
    14th La.
    15th La.

RODES' DIVISION
  Maj. Gen. Robert E. Rodes

Daniel's Brigade
  Brig. Gen. Junius Daniel***
  Col. Bryan Grimes

    32d N.C.
    45th N.C.
    53d N.C.
    2d N.C. Batt.

Ramseur's Brigade
  Brig. Gen. Stephen D. Ramseur

    2d N.C.
    4th N.C.
    14th N.C.
    30th N.C.

---

  * Reverted to two brigades 11 May 1864.
  ** WIA 10 May 1864
  *** Mortally Wounded in Action 12 May 1864.

Battle's Brigade
  Brig. Gen. Cullen A. Battle
    3d Ala.
    5th Ala.
    6th Ala.
    12th Ala.
    26th Ala.

Doles' Brigade
  Brig. Gen. George Doles
    4th Ga.
    12th Ga.
    44th Ga.

ARTILLERY
  Brig. Gen. Armistead Long

Braxton's Battalion
  Lt. Col. Carter Braxton
    Carpenter's (Va.) Batty.
    Cooper's (Va.) Batty.
    Hardwicke's (Va.) Batty.

Nelson's Battalion
  Lt. Col. William Nelson
    Kirkpatrick's (Va.) Batty.
    Massie's (Va.) Batty.
    Milledge's (Ga.) Batty.

Page's Battalion
  Maj. Richard C. Page
    Carter's, W.P. (Va.) Batty.
    Fry's (Va.) Batty.
    Page's (Va.) Batty.
    Reese's (Ala.) Batty.

Hardaway's Battalion
  Lt. Col. Robert A. Hardaway
    Dance's (Va.) Batty.
    Graham's (Va.) Batty.
    Griffin's, C.B. (Va.) Batty.
    Jones' (Va.) Batty.
    Smith's, B.H. (Va.) Batty.

Cutshaw's Battalion
  Maj. Wilfred E. Cutshaw

    Carrington's (Va.) Batty.
    Garber's, A.W. (Va.) Batty.
    Tanner's (Va.) Batty.

THIRD ARMY CORPS
Maj. Gen. Jubal Early

ANDERSON'S DIVISION
Brig. Gen. William Mahone

Perrin's Brigade
  Brig. Gen. Abner Perrin*

    8th Ala.
    9th Ala.
    10th Ala.
    11th Ala.
    14th Ala.

Mahone's Brigade
  Col. David A. Weisiger

    6th Va.
    12th Va.
    16th Va.
    41st Va.
    62st Va.

Harris' Brigade
  Brig. Gen. Nathaniel H. Harris

    12th Miss.
    16th Miss.
    19th Miss.
    48th Miss.

Wright's Brigade
  Brig. Gen. Ambrose R. Wright

    3d Ga.
    22d Ga.
    48th Ga.

---

* KIA 12 May 1864

2d Ga. Batt.

Perry's Brigade
Brig. Gen. Edward A. Perry
2d Fla.
5th Fla.
8th Fla.

HETH'S DIVISION
Maj. Gen. Henry Heth

Davis's Brigade
Brig. Gen. Joseph R. Davis
2d Miss.
11th Miss.
42d Miss.
55th N.C.

Cooke's Brigade
Brig. Gen. John R. Cooke
15th N.C.
27th N.C.
46th N.C.
48th N.C.

Walker's Brigade
Brig. Gen. Henry H. Walker*
22d Va.
40th Va.
47th Va.
55th Va.

Archer's Brigade
Brig. Gen. James J. Archer
13th Ala.
1st Tenn. (Provisional)
7th Tenn.
14th Tenn.

---

* WIA 10 May 1864

Kirkland's Brigade
  Brig. Gen. William W. Kirkland
    11th N.C.
    26th N.C.
    44th N.C.
    47th N.C.
    52d N.C.

WILCOX'S DIVISION
  Maj. Gen. Cadmus M. Wilcox

Lane's Brigade
  Brig. Gen. James H. Lane
    7th N.C.
    18th N.C.
    28th N.C.
    33d N.C.
    37th N.C.

McGowan's Brigade
  Brig. Gen. Samuel McCowan*
    Col. Joseph N. Brown
    1st S.C. (Provisional)
    12th S.C.
    13th S.C.
    14th S.C.
    1st S.C. (Orr's Rifles)

Scales' Brigade
  Brig. Gen. Alfred M. Scales
    13th N.C.
    16th N.C.
    22d N.C.
    34th N.C.
    38th N.C.

Thomas' Brigade
  Brig. Gen. Edward L. Thomas
    14th Ga.
    35th Ga.

---

* WIA 12 May 1864

45th Ga.
49th Ga.

Artillery
Col. R. Lindsey Walker

Poague's Battalion
Lt. Col. William T. Poague

Richard's (Miss.) Batty.
Utterback's (Va.) Batty.
Williams' (N.C.) Batty.
Wyatt's (Va.) Batty.

McIntosh's Battalion
Lt. Col. David R. McIntosh

Clutter's (Va.) Batty.
Donald's (Va.) Batty.
Hurt's (Ala.) Batty.
Price's (Va.) Batty.

Pegram's Battalion
Lt. Col. William J. Pegram

Brander's (Va.) Batty.
Cayce's (Va.) Batty.
Ellet's (Va.) Batty.
Marye's (Va.) Batty.
Zimmerman's (S.C.) Batty.

Richardson's Battalion
Lt. Col. Charles Richardson

Grandy's (Va.) Batty.
Landry's (La.) Batty.
Moore's (La.) Batty.
Penick's (Va.) Batty.

Cutt's Battalion
Col. Allen S. Cutts

Patterson's (Ga.)
Ross' (Ga.) Batt.
Wingfield's (Ga.) Batt.

Bibliography

By far the best study on the Spotsylvania Campaign thus far is the result of William D. Matter's exhaustive research, *If It Takes All Summer* (Chapel Hill, NC: 1988), extremely helpful to this author in understanding a confusing series of battles. Two good works for information on Grant's Overland Campaign from the Wilderness to Cold Harbor are Noah A. Trudeau's *Bloody Roads South* (Boston: 1988) and Gregory Jaynes' *The Killing Ground* (Alexandria, Va: 1986). The best biography on Lee is Douglas S. Freeman's multi-volume work *Robert E. Lee*, volume III of which covered the events in this book. Events viewed from Lee's staff can be found in Walter H. Taylor's *Four Years With General Lee* (NY: 1878)

Other books to read on the Spotsylvania campaign and used for this work are:

Ambrose, Stephen E. *Upton and the Army.* (Baton Rouge, LA: 1964)

Banes, Charles H. *History of the Philadelphia Brigade.* (Philadelphia, PA: 1876)

Blake, Henry N. *Three Years in the Army of the Potomac.* (Boston: 1865)

Bloodgood, J.D. *Personal Reminiscences of the War.* (New York: 1893)

Brown, Varina D. *A Colonel at Gettysburg and Spotsylvania.* (Columbia, SC: 1931)

Chamberlain, Thomas C. *History of the One Hundred and Fiftieth Pennsylvania Volunteers, Second Regiment, Bucktail Brigade.* (Philadelphia, PA: 1895)

Curtis, O.B. *History of the Twenty Fourth Michigan of the Iron Brigade.* (Detroit, MI: 1895)

Cushman, Frederick E. *History of the Fifty Eighth Massachusetts Volunteers.* (1865)

Fuller, Edward H. *Battles of the Seventy Seventh New York State Volunteers.* (Gloversville, 1901)

Gould, Joseph. *The Story of the Forty Eighth.* (Philadelphia, PA: 1908)

Haynes, F.M. *History of the Tenth Regiment, Vermont Volunteers.* (Lewiston, ME: 1870)

Bibliography

Haynes, Martin A. *A History of the Second Regiment New Hampshire Volunteer Infantry in the War of the Rebellion.* (Manchester, NH: 1865)

Hays, Gilbert A. *Under the Red Patch.* (Pittsburgh, PA: 1908)

Jackman, Lyman. *History of the 6th New Hampshire Regiment in the War for the Union.* (Concord, NH: 1891)

Lapham, William B. *My Recollections of the War of the Rebellion.* (Augusta, ME: 1892)

Lewis, Osceola. *History of the 138th Infantry Pennsylvania Volunteer Infantry.* (Norristown, PA: 1866)

Livermore, Thomas L. *Days and Events: 1860-1866.* (Boston, MA: 1920)

Lord, Edward O. *History of the Ninth Regiment New Hampshire Voun-teers in the War of the Rebellion.* (Concord, NH: 1895)

Marbaker, Thomas D. *History of the Eleventh New Jersey Volunteers.* (Trenton, NJ: 1898)

M'Bride, R.E. *In the Ranks from the Wilderness to Appomattox Court-house.* (Cincinatti, OH: 1891)

Mixson, Frank M. *Reminiscences of a Private.* (Columbia, SC: 1910)

Nash, Eugene. *A History of the Fourty Fourth Regiment New York Vol-unteer Infantry in the Civil War.* (Chicago: 1911)

Leon, Louis. *Diary of a Tar Heel Confederate Soldier.* (Charlotte, NC: 1913)

Long, A.L. *Memoirs of Robert E. Lee.* (New York: 1887)

Oates, William C. *The War Between the Union and the Confederacy.* (New York: 1905)

Page, Charles D. *History of the Fourteenth Regiment, Connecticutt Vol-unteer Infantry.* (Meridian, CT: 1906)

Powell, George R. *History of the Eighty Seventh Regiment Pennsylva-nia Volunteers.* (York, PA: 1901)

Powelson, B.F. *History of Company K of the 140th Regiment Pennsylva-nia Volunteers.* (Steubenville, OH: 1906)

Reed, William Howell, Ed. *War Papers of Frank P. Fay.* (Boston: 1911)

Roback, Henry. *The Veteran Volunteers of Herkimer and Otsego Coun-ties.* (Little Falls, NY: 1898)

Roe, Alfred S. *The Tenth Regiment Massachussetts Volunteer Infantry, 1861-1864.* (Springfield, MA: 1909)

Roe, Alfred S. *The Thirty Ninth Regiment Massachusetts Volunteer In-fantry, 1862-1865.* (Worcester, MA: 1914)

Santvoord, C. Van. *The One Hundred and Twenty Sixth Regiment New York State Volunteers.* (Roundout, NY: 1894)

Scott, Kate M. *History of the One Hundred and Fifth Regiment of Pennsylvania Volunteers.* (Philadelphia, PA: 1877)

Shaw, Horace H. *The First Maine Heavy Artillery, 1862-1865.* (Portland, ME: 1903)

Smith, A.P. *History of the Seventy Sixth Regiment New York Volunteers.* (Cortland, NY: 1867)

Smith, John Day. *The History of the Nineteenth Regiment of Maine Volunteer Infantry.* (Minneapolis, MN: 1909)

Staff, Louis M. *The Bohemian Brigade.* (New York, NY: 1954)

Stewart, Robert L. *History of the 140th Regiment of Pennsylvania Volunteers* (Philadelphia, PA: 1912)

Stiles, Robert. *Four Years with Marse Robert.* (New York: 1903)

Terrill, J. Newton. *Campaign of the 14th Regiment New Jersey Volunteers.* (New Brunswick, NJ: 1884)

Tyler, Mason W. *Recollections of the Civil War.* (New York: 1912)

Underwood, George C. *History of the Twenty-Sixth Regiment of North Carolina Troops in the Great War, 1861-1865.* (Goldsboro, NC: 1901)

Ward, Joseph R.C. *History of the 106th Regiment Pennsylvania Volunteers.* (Philadelphia, PA: 1906)

Washburn, George. *Military History and Record of the 108th Regiment New York Volunteers.* (Rochester, NY: 1894)

Welsch, Spencer G. *A Confederate Surgeon's Letters to His Wife.* (New York: 1911)

Williams, Sidney S. "From Spotsylvania to Wilmington, N.C. by Way of Andersonville and Florence." *Personal Narratives of Events in the War of the Rebellion.* (Providence, RI: 1899)

Willson, Arabella M. *Disaster, Struggle, Triumph.* (Albany, NY: 1870)

Worsham, John H. *One of Jackson's Foot Cavalry.* (New York: 1912)

Index